I've thoroughly enjoyed this meaty read
God's Word, has moments of the proph
today to be incarnational – identifying
our communities.
Gordon Tuck, Senior Pastor, Testwood Baptist Church

the
identification
principle

christopher
steed

how the incarnation shapes faith and ministry

INTER-VARSITY PRESS
36 Causton Street, London SW1P 4ST, England
Email: ivp@ivpbooks.com
Website: www.ivpbooks.com

First published 2019

British Library Cataloguing-in-Publication Data
A catalogue record for this book is available from the British Library.

ISBN: 978-1-78359-662-1
eBook ISBN: 978-1-78359-663-8

Set in Adobe Garamond 12/15 pt
Typeset in Great Britain by CRB Associates, Potterhanworth, Lincolnshire
Printed in Great Britain by Ashford Colour Press Ltd, Gosport, Hampshire

*Inter-Varsity Press publishes Christian books that are true to the Bible and that
communicate the gospel, develop discipleship and strengthen the church for its mission
in the world.*

*IVP originated within the Inter-Varsity Fellowship, now the Universities and Colleges
Christian Fellowship, a student movement connecting Christian Unions in universities
and colleges throughout Great Britain, and a member movement of the International
Fellowship of Evangelical Students. Website: www.uccf.org.uk. That historic association
is maintained, and all senior IVP staff and committee members subscribe to the UCCF
Basis of Faith.*

To all who have shared the journey
across the years

Contents

Preface

Living. The living God. The God who is alive with mysterious essence; the living God who refuses to meet us halfway. The living God who creates a new and living way through an action so profound it rings and resonates down the centuries. God who does not just exist but is thoroughly and fully alive, who comes to our level; to stoop, to embrace our existence and our very life; to conquer by force of love.

Loving. The loving God who refuses to compromise but who accommodates to the life we have to play out. Love that thus creates a drama by which every human life can be redeemed; love that penetrates human possibility with divine certainty. Loving, vast beyond imaginings, beyond intelligences; a mind beyond our imagination but vast with the vastness of the deepest ocean and far beyond. Love whose stupendous stoop of self-giving and the human embrace defines its essence.

Lighting. The God who alights here, alights in our midst to give light. A light more brilliant than a candle flame from whom the candle flames of human yearning have drawn. A light: the light of our times and of all times. A light, glowing in the darkness of injustice and of human rubbishing. A light enfolding with soft luminosity and transcendent strength.

Living, loving, lighting. A God who made himself known in the darkness of one dark night. Embodied, incarnated; being that comes to be with us, to be for us. Living, loving and lighting God who inserts himself into the folds of our humanity to be part of us, one of us, one with us; embrace of divine and human situation; solidarity locked in. Incarnation will save us. It did then; its radical implications will again.

Introduction

I take up this electronic pen 500 years after Luther criticized the church of his day. Never intending to spark a spiritual revolution, complete upheaval was far from the Reformer's mind. His social conservatism was at odds with the convulsions of pent-up forces that gathered around his revolution. Yet the spiritual and religious impetus that lay at its heart raised profound questions for his and every day.

'How can I find God?' 'How can I be rightly related to a God who strips away my pretensions with relentless searching and quizzical loving?' 'Should I just follow that which lies within me?' 'How does God see me now?' 'How can I find forgiveness to clear away the regrets that pile up like a car crash?'

Yet other questions press and impress, arising from the issues Luther drew back from. What about the great questions of today: questions of justice, of response to those who have no power, no food and no voice? The church has often stood by those who perpetrate violence and either just watched or cheered them on. Why should the left hand of the Reformation continue to be looked at askance by those who stress biblical authority? Why put up any more with privatized faith?

When I came on the Christian scene a generation ago, polarization ruled. Holding fast to the Bible meant little room for social concern outside of moral issues as then defined. Relevance is a never-ending and probably futile quest. Yet word is out that the church is irrelevant to the life of the world. Nevertheless, it continues doing what it does and succeeds in being both game and faithful. A full-blown and radical lens on the incarnation will save us from polarization and redeem us from irrelevance. Here's how.

Part One

Being incarnational . . .

I

While we slept (the landscape changed)

What is it that makes humans human? As science and technology challenge the boundaries between life and non-life, between organic and inorganic, this ancient question presses us hard.

What news of another world? What news of the future, of purpose and a shoreline? Someone is hailing us. He stood on the lake of Galilee once and calls to us again.

How shortsighted the church has been for so long. It has been unsure which way to face – whether towards the world or away from it. It has been unsure whether to emphasize talking to itself or to follow the path of mutual comprehension by learning to listen and talk. It has not been sure whether to emphasize individual sins or collective sins; personal pietism or social responsibility. Maybe we lacked the word range to talk to the life of the world. Our God, and our vocabulary, were too small. Unwitting captives to our culture, we could not speak to it, even when we prided ourselves on the independence of church and state.

The identification principle beckons to us to join the world as Jesus did (who combined messy involvement with critical radicalism and prophetic clarity). Either that or the church should at least listen and find out what is going on at ground level. The incarnation was profoundly world-affirming.

On this journey we will bring together two important ideas. The first is that Jesus represents God becoming part of our world, sharing its life and giving his. The second is that of the value of personhood. Our immense worth is divinely accredited. Incarnation is a complete immersion project into human experience, from manger to grave, culminating in the cross, Easter and beyond. In embracing it, Jesus endorsed our worth. Yet the incarnation, death and resurrection of Jesus are grounded in the idea that personhood has huge worth. The immense value of a human soul and the embrace of our bodily existence receive a vote of confidence.

That this is of vital relevance in our time is indisputable. Across the length and breadth of contemporary landscapes, human worth is a tumultuous storm centre. A liberal international order experiences profound culture quake; a certain view of the world is crumbling away. The stealthy march of voices of reason parading benign technology and unstoppable progress has been shown up. Science can promote many values. The mesh of reason, scientific triumph and betterment we call Enlightenment has always been prone to illiberal forces and illogical passions. There was always a dark side of hope. Yet our value, made in the mirror of God, can be the grounding of a new version of human flourishing.

Solidarity and imperceptible drift

At a philosophical level, I remain convinced that Christianity offers the 'best fit' between the scientific project and the inner psychological world.

Once, with no strong faith from family, and lacking personal previous convictions except atheism, I experienced encounter's power. Soon I was deeply touched with some wonderful truth. It was truth that set me longing and singing and soaring into God's skies, reaching upwards for an experience of holiness that was just out of my reach – or so it seemed. That was a generation ago. But societies don't sink, they change. What's happened in the meantime is that society and the church have drifted further and further apart. To be sure, the church has changed and taken on a style that would leave previous generations both uneasy and perplexed. But our general culture has altered vastly more and the gap has widened to the point where drowning people can hardly see the lifeboats.

They used to call it postmodernity and, while the term and its application are past their sell-by date, there is little doubt that a massive shift is occurring. Something is going on out there. We feel the impact, though it's difficult to grasp what we're dealing with. The change is a fundamental alteration in the landscape. And we noticed too late. We had been sleeping at the wheel. While we slept, the landscape changed. Take another look out of the window. People think differently, use words differently. Forget a view of the world based on progress. We are relational rather than rational. In its place is a touchy-feely, consumer approach to life where we pick and mix what works best for us.

While we have been asleep, much has happened. Some-one has moved the familiar landscapes around. Were we really

Rip Van Winkle? Have we been asleep that long? Prepare for re-entry!

The Tide is Running Out is an evocative title surveying the continuing fall-off in church attendance. In 'On Dover Beach', Matthew Arnold had little conception probably of a living personal faith, but 150 years later the tide was continuing to go out. We can protest that something good is happening on our stretch of the beach, and maybe we have scooped up a little bit of water and go running down back and forward to the sea. Small local successes and a trickle here and there blind us to the bigger picture. Despite countless cries that we can see approaching waves of revival, the tide is still going out across the beach generally. The simple truth is that people go anywhere and everywhere in their spiritual search (that is as strong as ever) but prefer junk food to the bread of life.

The caller and the call

A new approach is needed. More of the same will not work.

For there is a call going out that many are hearing. While we slept and the landscape out there was subtly assuming different contours, a call was being left on our answerphone. While we got on with our own thing on our little stretch of the beach, someone was hailing us. The caller was the Lord.

The theme of this book is how the identification principle plays out in relation to the immense value of the human being. We will trace it through various pathways and show how the wider question of the worth of persons generally can both inspire worship of the Worthy One as well as clarify the incarnation and such theological issues as atonement and justification. We will be miners, mining the theme of incarnation for how much its radical implications shape practice: the very craft of ministry.

Among these implications is the call to social transform-
ations. Until recent times, the church has not talked much
about challenging the system. Surely we can get on with
helping the vulnerable without going down that road?
Transforming society, though, is the extension of ministry to
those who are without. How can you care about the poor
without caring about the poverty that produces them? How
can you care for the slave without indignation against the
noxious racism that generated it?

The message is simple and straightforward. It is to re-engage
with the world and yet do so holistically rather than in a
polarized way. It is a call we have heard many times and have
wondered what it means and what the boundaries are. Many
insistent voices have picked up this message and brought it to
us. But this time we want to hear it and understand what we
are to do.

As battle approached with the French and Spanish fleets on
an October morning in 1805, Admiral Nelson ordered his
famous signal: 'England confides that every man will do
his duty.' Mr Pascoe, the Signal Lieutenant, was to run up the
message quickly because Nelson had a further signal to make
almost immediately. Mr Pascoe begged leave to substitute the
word 'expects' for 'confides' because 'expects' was the first word
in the Signal Book and would save several hoists. To this
suggestion, the Admiral readily agreed. 'That will do, make
it directly,' he ordered. As soon as 'England expects' was
placarded and received to thunderous 'three cheers' in every
ship, the next signal was quickly substituted. It was number
16, the signal for close action. 'Engage the enemy more
closely.' Number 16 remained at the topgallant masthead of
the *Victory* until shot away.

'Engage the enemy more closely!' And, to be sure, we must
engage the enemy more closely, but the summons goes beyond

spiritual warfare. In the roar and smoke of battle, number 16 is still fluttering. The summons to re-engage and not withdraw is an urgent call to the church. But what does it mean?

Communicate we must. Over the years the church has lost so much ground; a revolution has been steadily advancing in communications. Though incremental to its participants, spectators would observe a whirring speed of change that has accelerated through the 1960s, 70s, 80s and 90s, and roared into the millennium. Once, telephones sat on desks or were glued to the wall. Computers were a rumour put about by geeks in the room down the corridor. Now personal communicators are a cosmetic on the ears of the public everywhere you go. Inexorably, computers were in every home and began to talk to each other. It was the birth of the internet, the most astounding means of communication since prayer started. It is the era of high-speed connection.

One thing seems certain. For the most part, people won't be coming into Christian churches. They won't come to hear magnificent preaching or be dazzled by our music – not necessarily because they choose not to, but because it won't occur to them in the first place. If the people won't come up the mountain, we must go down to engage with them where they are. This is the identification principle. It is what Jesus did as he came to serve, thereby demonstrating astonishing affinity for what it is to be human as well as bringing God-level presence. We will press the radical implications of this.

In taking to himself a new identity and wrapping himself in the curious garb of our tattered humanity, Jesus gave a vote of confidence to that very means of expression. It proclaims in unmistakable ring tones that what it means to be human is something he lovingly embraces. As the writer to the Hebrew Christians puts it in texts we will need to explore, 'what are human beings that you are mindful of them, or mortals, that you care for them? You have made them only a little lower than the angels; you have crowned them with glory and honour' (Hebrews 2:6–7, NRSV, invoking Psalm 8). Then comes the statement that is like high explosive. It is this very identity that Jesus has taken. The statement made is celebrated wherever Christians sing their hymns, wherever creeds are recited or theology articulated. Yet the consequences often lie hidden in rubble.

The church does not really believe in the value of humanity, so affirmed by its Lord in riotous whisperings. It cannot, or it would have behaved differently. Between rhetoric and reality is a great gulf fixed. If we really believed in the immense value borne by our fellows, how we do church would look and feel very different. We would tread softly with respect to their ·sacred value (while doubly indignant in the face of desecrating injustice). We would have no truck with racism or gender violence.

Jesus has so spectacularly embraced and affirmed the value and worth that humans have. That is not, though, the starting point for our journey – that is the worth of God. Humans have immense value placed upon them because they are replicas of God. Valuable in our own right, it is nevertheless a bequeathed and reflected glory, as the moon is to the sun. Humans are valued highly since they reflect upon the glory of something that is most highly prized of all. God the Lord is the source of value and worth, supremely worthy and the creator of meaning placed on personal beings such as ourselves. It is in his light that we see light. It is in the worthiness of God who holds us in his gaze that we see our own worth, a recognition of our own value marred by actions and pervasive attitudes that render us unworthy. This is the journey we will take.

The journey begins

First milestone. Personal beings have immense value, which is true of humans and even more so of the source of all value, namely God, who is transcendent and worthy of worth-ship. This is far from a philosophical puzzle. To ignore God is to disrespect; to devalue and deface is a serious business.

Second milestone. God is the guarantor of human value and worth on account of creation. Just as in human endeavours, the worth of a creator is invested in a worthwhile task; we have high value that comes from God seeing us in a certain light. The creation is a divinely shaped sphere of life.

Third milestone. In the unrepeatable incarnation, Jesus expresses solidarity with our situation, identifying as human *with us and for us* and then as universal victim. The embrace of embodiment came with all its ambiguity. Yet at heart this is the return of the king, who comes to re-establish the reign of Israel's God, but whose return from the grave brings human redemption.

Fourth milestone. Dishonouring people was well understood in the honour culture within which much of the Bible was framed. Ancient cultures, and many contemporary societies also, work on the principle of honour and shame (maximizing the one, reducing the other). Beyond doubt, that is a thread that runs through the Bible. We see Jesus counteracting the social shame of the Samaritan woman, of lepers and the marginalized. But not valuing others, through disrespect, indifference or indignity, is a social dynamic common to human affairs. It is the essence of sin. The demand for recompense arises in everyday life when personal value is rubbished or demeaned (God is also affected).

Fifth milestone. The cross is the meeting point between heaven and earth, the clearing house for recompense and indebtedness. Forget talk of punishing the innocent. Beyond the sacrificial system that for the most part is a far cry from our own times is the idea that a price must always be paid. God's answer – *tetelestai* (John 19:30) – was written on receipts in New Testament times to show a bill had been paid in full.

Sixth milestone. 'Trading places' (switching positions) is central both to human life and to scenes of violence. At the cross, an exchange takes place. At the messy violence that shows the depth of the divine–human encounter, there is somewhere to go. The result is 'justification', a truth that is more than just one part of the armoury of Christian doctrine; it is internally related to all truths of faith.

All this will be well-trodden ground, though the ideas expressed are perhaps clothed in different garb. Our route takes us past Himalayan peaks we can barely glance. Talk of creation, its whys and hows, can only be noted in passing. Talk of election and how a universal faith might emerge from the particularity of a chosen people cannot detain us long. Why a universal God chooses one people, and where such exceptionalism leaves everyone else, is beyond the scope of this slender volume.

We will have to move on to the radical implications of this lens for the embodiment of divine love. There are, we will explore, four ways of being incarnational today: intercession, anointed apologetic, loving service and social transformation, and then the continuing presence of God through his church.

We're going to take a fresh look at how we re-engage with the world through a particular lens. It is a lens that concentrates the burning glory of God's Son into a point that makes an impact. It is a lens that will enable us to see with clarity what God is asking of us at this time. The lens that will give us such focus is the identification of Jesus with us, the staggering way that God became a human being for a brief moment in history. 'They will call him Immanuel – which means, "God with us"' (Matthew 1:23). *With* – it is a word pregnant with immense power.

This is the message of the New Testament. God has become with us and one of us. Jesus became our brother and stood in solidarity with sinful, suffering humanity. As we hear the call that is going out to the Christian church, we follow the progress of the Son of God as he joined himself to the human condition, immersing himself into what it means to be human and treading the lonely road to Calvary. We look again at the way the human experiences of Jesus give him insider knowledge of what it means to be human. We catch a glimpse of Jesus as the sin-bearer and the one who bears our sorrows (every one). We feel the impact of being joined up to his resurrection.

It is the identification principle. Identification is common enough in our lives here. We identify with a life situation in a TV soap, a football team, a place, a faith and a nation. All define us and locate our lives. Identifying with our country is a powerful form of belonging, though not to be confused with a dangerous nationalism that upholds my country right or wrong, as inherently superior to yours.

Notwithstanding oceans of ink about the incarnation of Jesus, we have more to fathom about the staggering immersion of God in the communal solidarity of what it means to be human. Jesus embodied the empathy of God, an empathy with the human situation that not only liberates us personally but is a sign of how we are to follow on. It was the empathy of God that took Jesus into active identification with the human condition. Jesus did not beam down and join the human race as an alien, an outsider. He was born into it and became the insider. Only this way was he able to become the liberator and saviour of the human race. His humanity was not a shell; neither were his human experiences faked. Because he was real God and a real man, Jesus is therefore in a position to offer decisive help generously to anyone who applies for it genuinely.

As the letter to the Hebrews puts it:

> Therefore he had to become like his brothers and sisters in every respect, so that he might be a merciful and faithful high priest in the service of God, to make a sacrifice of atonement for the sins of the people. Because he himself was tested by what he suffered, he is able to help those who are being tested. (2:17–18, NRSV)

Jesus helps us not by looking on but by getting in there with us. He still does that through his active presence, his living Holy Spirit. The time of his appearing was brief. One and now another millennium have passed. Still there is someone in the heavens pleading his cause and ours and waiting with arms outstretched for each generation to embrace it and make it theirs.

Much has happened in our generation and we are still here, trying to work out what it means to be a disciple of Jesus and what it means to be the church. At times we seem stuck, unable to break out of our background sufficiently to re-engage with it as missionaries. Yet there is a longing in the church, a longing too great to allow us to sink quietly with forlorn hope and the disillusioned shreds of failed prophecy. We are like those on the road to Emmaus: 'We had hoped that he was the

one who was going to redeem Israel. And what is more, it is
the third day since all this took place' (Luke 24:21).

But there is one who is walking alongside us because he
always does. That is his custom. Just as Jesus walked alongside
two confused disciples, he trod the same ground as every one
of us does, in suffering solidarity and triumphant empathy.
The same one who walked with humanity walks with us today
through his Spirit and urges us to walk with the world and
show them a way out of the sunset of broken dreams and into
the sunrise of hope. 'The Christ will suffer and rise from the
dead on the third day, and repentance and forgiveness of sins
will be preached in his name to all nations, beginning at
Jerusalem. You are witnesses of these things' (Luke 24:46–48).

Wanted for our era: people who can understand the life and
times of the world and who can speak to it with an unbeatable
combination of sensitivity and authority; those who bear
congenial witness yet leave no doubt where we are coming
from and the stance we take.

Walking with biblical faithfulness alongside the world in its
messy, muddled pain, the identification principle calls us to
get alongside contemporary people and relate to them. The
God of our journey will go with us as we walk this road and
as we allow the empathy of God to make a fresh impact on us
and turn us inside out. It will refresh us as we walk, confident
of the final victory and triumph of the Lamb.

2

Worship (for all God's worth)

This book is about reconnecting with the world around us. For some unchurched people who think they've heard it all before, it will be a reconnection. For others, it will be a fresh connection.

We can get confused. Across the years, many voices beckoned us in what seems to be a different direction in order to make the greatest impact on the world, recover our lost position and win a lost world. Many calls are made to learn what is so amazing about grace, to seek the face of God in prayer, pray for revival, and especially to be passionate about discipleship and personal holiness.

These are good calls, right calls. We cannot make a difference unless we are different. We cannot effect change unless we are changed. This is where personal holiness comes in. Holiness means to be separate, to be other, to be set apart, sanctioned and dedicated. When Isaiah was caught off guard by the glare of God's brightness, he became aware that this was the Holy One of Israel and that his personal walk with God could no more be relied upon than a paper boat would suffice for crossing the Pacific Ocean. The gulf between Isaiah and the Creator of the universe was suddenly far wider than he had supposed. 'Holy, holy, holy,' he responds with mounting alarm, 'the whole earth is full of your glory.' In that terrifying, illusion-shattering moment, Isaiah realized that the living God was so transcendent in shining glory and so incredibly holy that the only recourse was to fall on the mercy of God without delay or pretence. Isaiah had accidently stumbled on the God he had been serving, and now he was unhinged for ever, like a door that will not fit back on its mountings properly. He had gazed on the source of holiness: every word he had ever spoken now seemed foolish and unclean.

The holiness of God is a contrast on two scales of measurement. There is a vast contrast in size. The Creator knows what is going on right now in the quasars at the edge of the universe. Sometimes we do not know what is going on in our own family. We are at the mercy of the elements. The Creator made the elements. But there is another scale besides the contrast between being finite and infinite. It is the moral gap between the source of holiness and the professional sinner; the difference in holy brightness that is like a fading torch compared to the yellow star we are parked near. This is the gulf that Isaiah now realizes he can never cross even if he were to try until his days were done. The barrier is un-crossable. Maybe angels could do it, but human beings do not stand an earthly chance. And this is the pattern throughout the Old Testament whenever the curtain is drawn back for a prophet.

But seven hundred years later, it was a different era. We are in a different movement of history and of how God relates to the world. Isaiah and fellow prophets see a tiny part of the transcendent God who is far above in every possible way. Little did he suspect that one day God would step off his throne and come down to his level. We are in a period that began when the Creator became one of the human race and identified himself with us. Though this phase is drawing to a close, still we are caught up in the identification movement of God's dealing with the world. The Creator is no longer just the transcendent being who dwells the other side of the curtain and demands that we come to him. Isaiah's God has stepped out to forge a deep connection with the world that rejected him.

Seeking the face of a holy God is not optional for us. Spending unhurried time with God and finding an oasis in our everyday life is a daily necessity for twenty-first-century disciples rushing through a fast-paced world. Discipleship in the way of God, learning to be his people once again, is a command not a suggestion. But so often we continue to polarize on these vital issues. We hear a call to connect with the world and wonder how it all hangs together. 'Not another issue I need to know about,' we groan, and one more burden is added to our already burdened lives or creaking church programme.

Here is good news. There is no rivalry between competing concerns. The road map in front of us suggests how we might *go* into all the world. To 'go' is the flip side of the call in the other direction, to *come*. It was the apostle and remains the high priest of our profession who sends us out in this rhythm (Hebrews 3:1). God's profoundly personal identification with our humanity sets a pattern.

The radical implications of the incarnation involve what we term the 'identification principle'. We bring together worship, humanity, atonement, proclamation of the cross and of accept-ance. In the same bracket, we take in such matters as social engagement, intercession, empathy and mission.

These concerns are often split asunder. We are cultural captives but lack the capacity to speak into the culture that

mes from immersive worship (plus a healthy bit of
cal reflection). To paraphrase Martin Luther, 'If you
r   the gospel in all aspects with the exception of the
issues that deal specifically with your time, you are not
preaching the gospel at all.' Yet what God has joined together
let no-one put asunder. That is what the post-millennial
church should be doing: making connection. Making a
stronger connection with where our hearers are; making
a connection with battered people, connecting with those
who are trapped, making a connection through passionate
intercession, connecting with the lonely and lost; bringing
insight that is deeply biblical, the only witness to the incarnation on offer. Without this, the church looks like a strange
tribe that modernity left behind.

We start with God. His name is dishonoured, ignored,
often forgotten on the cutting-room floor of memory. It was
lament for this that the psalmist agonized over, pleading for
its revival. As we move into a new type of society in the West,
characterized by networked individuals and 'voice and choice',
it is important to stress that most cultures in biblical times
were defined by social honour. Disgrace on clan or family
brought shame. Ancient cultures and many contemporary
societies also work on the principle of honour and shame
(maximizing the one, reducing the other). Beyond doubt, that
is a thread through the Bible. We see Jesus counteracting
the social shame of the Samaritan woman, of lepers and the
marginalized. 'The honour of God' has been brought into
disrepute with Islamic fundamentalism, yet divine worth is
central to the concerns of Scripture. God can also be devalued.
Giving God the honour due to his name is vital to worship
and Christian liturgy. It was emphasized much in the Reformation. 'Let God be God!' Divine worth is about worship,
'worthship'. To worship is to accord worth, to recognize

something as being of highest and truest value, to recognize
and give respect to the highest worth it has.

A crescendo of worthship goes on every day – but not necessarily in church or cathedral. This world worships continually;
we were created to do so. We worship what we believe to be
worth it – sports, prestige, power, material possessions, relationships, vices, recreation; the list is endless. And all of these
things get our passion, our reverent love, our life. Is what we
are worshiping truly worth it? Falsities that evoke potent desire
– money, sex and power – will enslave and make us less worthy.

Ascribing greatness to God and offering him devoted adoration and total outpouring of praise is not only due, it is
entirely appropriate. God must be honoured.

> I will proclaim the name of the LORD;
>> ascribe greatness to our God!
> The Rock, his work is perfect,
>> and all his ways are just.
> A faithful God, without deceit,
>> just and upright is he.
> (Deuteronomy 32:3–4, NRSV)

The writer of the Song of Moses is declaring the rightness of
ascribing greatness and proclaiming the name of Yahweh not
as an abstract principle but because of action: the acts of
Yahweh played out in the nation's history and in law-giving.
God the Lord is no supreme tyrant, a cruel despot commanding
obedience, or an arbitrary dictator. Yahweh acts according to
fair principles, consistently, righteously.

Why is God the supremely Worthy One (as many hymns
attest in contrast with our unworthiness)? Simply because he
is the ultimate, but is fair rather than arbitrary. It would not
be appropriate to award such full-hearted praise and total

adoration to human beings. Greatness and praise are to be accorded to a God who has been active on our behalf. More than this, if that were possible, God the Lord is beautiful and the source of all beauty (for wonder and worship walk together). As the psalms evoke:

> One thing I ask of the LORD,
>   this is what I seek:
> that I may dwell in the house of the LORD
>   all the days of my life,
> to gaze upon the beauty of the LORD
>   and to seek him in his temple.
> (Psalm 27:4)

> And let the beauty of the LORD our God be upon us: and establish thou the work of our hands upon us; yea, the work of our hands establish thou it. (Psalm 90:17, KJV)

Psalm 145 gives full expression to a God who is beyond all human comparison; the Lord who is over all, separate and distinct from all yet involved and committed:

> All your works shall give thanks to you, O LORD,
>   and all your faithful shall bless you.
> They shall speak of the glory of your kingdom,
>   and tell of your power.
> (Psalm 145:10–11, NRSV)

The remaining psalms summon sun and moon, mountains and hills, creatures of sea and land to give enthusiastic praise; though not consciously mobilized, they fulfil the law of their being. Unconscious worship is recruited from the wonder of the world. Then at the close of the Bible comes the finale – the making of music by enthusiastic, conscious people who know what they are doing and why.

> You are worthy, our Lord and God,
>   to receive glory and honour and power,
> for you created all things,
>   and by your will they existed and were created.
> (Revelation 4:11, NRSV)

> You are worthy to take the scroll
>   and to open its seals,
> for you were slaughtered and by your blood you ransomed
>   for God
> saints from every tribe and language and people and nation.
> (Revelation 5:9, NRSV)

In his visions, the Seer of Patmos is gripped by an overwhelming sense of the God who is worthy, supremely worthy. As the Creator and originator of all that is, God is worthy to receive honour and glory. Then the scenery shifts. The Lamb appears, holding the scroll of the future. That occasions a fresh paeon of praise. An overwhelming sense of worthiness is directed now towards the figure known as the Lamb. The praise song is taken up; living creatures and church leaders in their myriads sing with a loud and full voice that is utterly compelling: 'Worthy, worthy' – is the one who holds human worth in the palm of his hand and confers meaning on his creation.

Then the song changes slightly:

> Worthy is the Lamb that was slaughtered
> to receive power and wealth and wisdom and might
> and honour and glory and blessing!
> (Revelation 5:11, NRSV)

In the visions of the Seer of Patmos, it is the Lamb who is worthy. The glory of Christ shines out in the great work of redemption he has accomplished on the earth. To him belongs due 'power and wealth and wisdom and might and honour and glory and blessing'. Christians today have less of a sense of 'the glory of Christ'. It used to be a main theme of biblical exposition and theological writing – for instance the outstanding work of that title by the Puritan writer John Owen.

'Worship' is a word that comes from Anglo Saxon. 'Worthship' was to give honour and due where required. In Old English spelling, 'worthship' meant that the greater the *worth* something had, the greater the honour or renown should be given. This had meaning for a society that was becoming increasingly feudal, a society in strict layers requiring honour and homage in exchange for protection and land. To the Anglo-Saxons, that was valid and appropriate at every ascending level.

Ascribing worth is appropriate for personal beings of any kind. They are worthy because valuable. They ought not to be rubbished or ridden over. How much more the living God who inhabits the fullest being? How much more the Creator and Redeemer who is the Lord of heaven and earth? That is the standpoint of the book of Revelation. Ultimately victorious over every other potentate, the Lamb holds the key to the unfolding future. The great acts of the Lamb in recent history attest to that.

The essence of what 'worship' means in the Greek language is *proskuneo*, 'to kiss the hand toward'. The one who offers the kiss of the hand believes that the other is truly worth adoring.

The worth of God and the source of value

God, the Lord of heaven and earth is supremely worthy of the devotion and service of humanity. The living God is just that, the living God. Neither a force nor an alien spirit, nor an amorphous presence, God is the ultimate personal being and the source of value and meaning that validates personhood.

There can be no divorce between love of God and love of others as its authentic overflow. 'You shall love the Lord your God with all . . . You shall love your neighbour as yourself.' The one is inseparable from the other. We bring into our worship our love and responsibilities to neighbour. We bring love for God as the supreme value into our love and service.

It is a question for philosophy. Where does the value and worth of humans derive from? How is it that from scientific laws as we comprehend them, people like ourselves make astonishing claims about their significance. How dare we assert our value in the teeth of a universe that is at best unfeeling, at worst despotically indifferent? Modern people are inhabitants of two worlds. We accept (with caution) results of a scientific understanding of reality as it develops. Yet there is an interior life, an interpersonal life, an emotional world we are compelled to work with (or disregard at our peril).

We have here surely a strong argument for the question that has exercised the ages, God's existence. As the thirsty crave water, humans need a healthy dose of valuing in order to thrive. A valuing environment is crucial for people like us. Without it we wither. Yet what is the source of the value we must have? An impersonal universe? Blind, random forces acting in self-replicating systems? How has a universe constructed on these principles generated personal beings that simply have to have value – or face the consequences?

The qualities humans need to flourish are central to the universe. We are compelled to live as if truth, human value, faithfulness, justice and love are but incidental to the science story about the nature of things. But is the world completely blind and deaf to the things we prize and long for? Whatever point and purpose in the universe, does it not include our consciousness, our purpose, our dignity and beauty? Why, we must plead, why should we remain separated from the source of our lives, who alone can impart the meaning and direction we seek and explain us to ourselves? There is someone out there who corresponds to what is in here. The Creator spoken of in the Bible embodies those qualities of truth and love humans need in order to thrive, a God of faithfulness and justice. His is that purpose in the universe that imparts our worth in our personhood, in our individuality, that recognizes our creativity as a mirror of his artistry. And the Creator is a God whose will is the yardstick of right and wrong, who is opposed to the world's corruption but who will cleanse us.

We say to the people of our times, 'We know why we are fashioned as you are. We know why we have value and from whence arises the indignant protest when that is trampled on and discarded.'

For us to live in our world, we are desperate to have our value upheld – not just philosophers but all of us. With it, we flourish; without it, we wither. Few of us – even mocking atheists or aggressive scientists – will be inwardly silent in the face of indifference (being neither seen nor heard). Few of us will be comfortable with being diminished, cut down to size, or being meted out unequal treatment. Few of us will not react in the presence of indignity. Our value cries out in the night.

Human worth and significance do not, though, live by themselves. We need others to give us that meaning. Those around us in the sphere in which we live, move and have our being are needed to affirm our value. Those who live independently of what others think are either liars, completely amoral or spoilt children; endlessly parading their rights or the psychopathic primacy of their immense thoughts. Someone who endorses the silent meaning of our lives is crucial. We are, let it be said, creatures of interaction, of an interpersonal life, and responsibilities to our fellows. A community of valuers is our meat and drink.

God the Lord of cosmos and of the blue planet with its strange inhabitants looks upon us and validates our value. In his face, we see our face; marred but with a glimmer of hope. His worth is the ultimate endorsement that our personhood has value, that our sigh and cry are worthwhile because we are worthwhile. To have value there needs to be a valuer, one whose recognition brings life.

For the honour of God? (The dark side)

The incarnation radically affirms the value of the means chosen for God to make himself known – our tattered and dishevelled humanity. What it means to be human has been honoured by the honour of God. But the honour of God has been dis-honoured by those who dishonour people.

There is a dark side. The power of this dark side has been growing in our day. It lies with those who seek to cite the worth and honour of God not as a source of the worth of humanity but its opposite.

When radical clerics sought to stir young men and women into radical action and Islamic Jihad, leaving them with unholy fire in their eyes but heavy with a sense of obligation; when the logic of that action pointed inexorably towards violence being acceptable and then mandatory; when suicide bombers were dispatched on their mission to fulfil such a logic, we might well ask, 'Where are the voices that challenged why they thought Allah had demanded such a chilling dis-regard for human life?'

Yet pitting the best of Christianity against the worst of other religions is not only unfair, it leaves us smug and complacent. Christian history has a dark past that has not yet had its day. Its callous disregard for people's lives can show a chasm between doctrine and practice.

The USA, known for its religious and social conservatism, witnessed enormous violence at the junction where religiosity and slavery met, and this shapes attitudes today. Underpinned by religious faith, a racial caste system defined its existence until the Civil War. It found its aftermath in the gruesome story of domestic violence in the form of lynch mobs, an ugly episode in national history. The most unsettling reality of this lynching is the degree to which white Americans embraced it, not as an uncomfortable necessity or a way of maintaining order but as a joyous moment and a family day out: 'Girls giggled as the flies fed on the blood that dripped from the Negro's nose,' as one newspaper reported in 1930.[1] And all this was scarcely challenged by evangelical churches through to the 1950s.

The church colluded with any form of so-called 'justice' in that situation, and in dark episodes such as the Rwandan genocide more recently. The record of sexual abuse is another signpost to a region we wish wasn't there, for it is both past and present. The dreadful deeds that have taken place in religious establishments responsible for teaching, instructing or caring for children over the generations are wretched. Perpetrators hiding in churches have wreaked huge damage on countless numbers of children, physically, emotionally and morally.

It is not just horrific crimes like this that have stained the Christian church and, for instance, marginalized it in Ireland. There are any number of self-righteous, self-appointed judges who bind others with their traditions and their legalism and who cry foul when their grim-faced legacy is challenged. The freedom and fullness of divine grace has yet to liberate their souls.

It is not good enough that in an honour culture, people defend family honour to the extent of dishonouring and rubbishing the lives of those who have infringed. God can defend his own honour. God's name being dishonoured is a real issue. But not like this. Divine worth must be affirmed in a worthwhile way. It can no longer be separated from upholding the value of people.

Between rhetoric and reality there is a great gulf fixed. The problem lies in our incomplete doctrine. It is also in our blind spot when it comes to the power of power. Fixing it is not the work of a day or a year.

The glory that dazzles (The power of the light side)

The glory that dazzles is a theme of the writer to the Hebrew Christians endeavouring to show that Jesus Christ is the fulfilment of Old Testament priest, temple and sacrifice. He is 'the real'; those visual expressions of what it meant to draw close to God in the Old Testament period were but shadow.

Paul's high view of Jesus is expressed most notably in Ephesians, Philippians and Colossians – the prison epistles. It was in captivity that he was overcome and taken up with the One he has served through enormous struggle and whom he adores with wholehearted love and devotion. His statements about Christ are not to be seen as mere theology divorced from the heart. They are the fruit of worship, an outpouring of emotional cognition and reasoning. Paul is not a spectator.

The glory of Christ, Paul adds in Ephesians and Colossians, is about his hidden role in the creation of everything, as well as the overt role in restoring broken humanity. For Paul, as much as Patmos's much-tested Seer, the glory that dazzles is not merely the shining of any radiant being. It expresses the uniqueness of Christ. There is no-one else who commands such attention and significance. Alone among earthly and spiritual beings, Jesus has brought about vast and magnificent achievement.

From the standpoint of Scripture, the honour and worthship due to God have important implications for how people live their lives and what they prioritize. They are the foundation of the idea of atonement. This is not a book about how the doctrine of the incarnation has been understood by Christians of former ages so much as a fresh look at the implications of this astounding message. But we ought to note that in trinitarian theology, for God to identify himself with the human race required the second person of the Godhead. The Holy Spirit could not do this particular job, nor could the Father. It is the Son who came to identify with us. The early Christian father Tertullian was right. It is incorrect to imply that the Father was crucified. It was not the Father who came to identify with us.

To create the universe and fine-tune the balance of forces with pinpoint precision required a mind beyond our imagination: the very self-expression of the mind of God, embodied on earth. 'In the beginning was the Word' (John 1:1, NRSV). 'And the Word became flesh and lived among us' (John 1:14, NRSV). He assumed human form and took a flesh-and-blood human body. Just as a word is the expression of our inner thought, the Word is the self-expression of the Father. The Word gave form to the entire universe, speaking out the thoughts and will of God. Is this not what the mysterious Colossians 1:15–16 is getting at? 'He is the image of the invisible God, the firstborn over all creation. For by him all things were created: things in heaven and on earth.' In the image culture of today, this is intriguing.

A Christian philosophy of the created sphere can offer a solution to the so-called 'participant problem', that things only exist when we observe them, or that the act of our observation calls a given outcome into question. This is the imponderable dilemma of quantum physics, that the universe would be nothing without being observed. But it does exist! It exists in the act of seeing by God, in the very mind and in the beholding by the Creator whose vision is life-giving.

All the forms in the mind of God were expressed and shaped by the Word, who formed the mould of the cosmos. With the genome project and the internet revolution racing away, we could now say: 'In the beginning was an information processing system; in the beginning was an instruction coded into every cell of every living thing . . . in the beginning was the programmer who became part of his own programme.' Is this not what John found so startling, that the Word who had spoken the worlds into being, who gave form to everything, had been spoken into our world and taken human form? 'Without him nothing was made that has been made' (John 1:3).

Athanasius was the fourth-century Christian writer who saved Christianity from becoming something else. With a passion, Athanasius waged a guerrilla war against the Trinity deniers of his day. 'Can you really think', he asks, 'that there was a time when the Father was without his Word, his expression?' The Logos runs deep, into the very nature of God. The Son is co-equal and has always been. It says something profound that the Word is represented in the relationship of a Son to the Father. 'The Father loves the Son and has placed everything in his hands' (John 3:35). One cannot digest all the statements Jesus made about the Father and the Son without realizing that this is an eternal relationship. The Son is not some created being, or the first being to be created. This would place him as a sort of angel, and you end up with two gods. The link between the Father and the Son is primary, intrinsic to God's very nature.

'Father, the time has come. Glorify your Son . . . that all of them
may be one, Father, just as you are in me and I am in you . . .
that they may be one as we are one . . . you loved me before the
creation of the world . . . I have made you known to them, and will
continue to make you known in order that the love you have for
me may be in them and that I myself may be in them.' (John 17)

It very much looks from Scripture as if this is the primary
relationship in the Godhead: 'Grace, mercy and peace from
God the Father and Christ Jesus our Lord' (1 Timothy 1:2).
We can read this as a standard way of saying hello without
realizing that it is rooted in an eternal principle. Just as within
a family children are brought into the primary relationship,
so within God there is a loving and eternal bond between the
Father and the Son. Unity and relationships characterize
divinity. God was not a lonely, isolated deity and did not need
to build a family. Before the creation of the universe, there was
relationship: a relationship that is a living personal principle.
It is the ground of a valuing relationship within human community. This is fundamentally why we are relational beings.

The Creator is infinite. There can be no room for more than
one infinite spirit. Look above us, at the mighty universe.
Then peer inside at the conscious mind. The Creator is the
common ground both of the rationality of our minds and of
the whole universe. Perfect uniformity and agreement of all
its forces and parts point to one cause behind all things. A
single pattern in the universe counts against the idea of many
competing gods. One set of laws, one set of building materials,
one God.

Should it surprise us that the dimensions of a Being who
spans time and space are on a very different plane from what
our minds can conceive? The central, underlying principle of
the universe is not survival, fate, chaos or chance, but close

relationship: a community of love, divine love realized within the Creator. This is the principle underlying the totality of the world – and our own inner life. It is the ground and being of our personhood that cries out to be honoured.

Whether it be amid the honour culture of the biblical world or of any era, the living God is worthy of maximum honour, of fullest praise. God is offered adoration and praise that would not befit human beings. 'Worthship' is entirely appropriate.

Humans, made in God's image, deserve respect and validation in their dignity. This flows from ascribing ultimate value and worth to the Creator.

Show me what kind of a God you worship, and the kind of humanity you possess will stand out.

'*The true position of mankind as no mere atom of the infinite but a finite reproduction of his maker is likely to stand and will stand, unshaken.*'
William D. McLaren[1]

'*At the beginning, mankind was formed in the image and resemblance of God so that he might admire his Maker in the dignity with which God had so nobly invested him and might honour him with appropriate thankfulness.*'
John Calvin[2]

3

Children of the sixth day: the God of our humanity

On a clear night, we can see for ever. The sight is irresistible: garden lights strung across the emptiness of space, layer after layer of star upon star as far as the eye can see. Tiny sparks of light, as fine as rain on a windscreen at night. Fiery worlds: a torchlit procession of silent participants whose parade stretches into endless distance. What would it be like to stand on the edge of the universe to gaze into the unknown and uncharted? The estate just goes on and on.

We are the beings that must fathom ourselves and our place in the scheme of things. Can we really maintain human significance in a universe that goes on and on without end?

'To whom will you compare me?
  Or who is my equal?' says the Holy One.
Lift your eyes and look to the heavens:
  Who created all these?
He who brings out the starry host one by one,
  and calls them each by name.

Because of his great power and mighty strength,
    not one of them is missing.
(Isaiah 40:25–26)

For three centuries, astronomers had pondered those little luminous wisps between the stars. Were they Catherine wheels of swirling gas? But maybe they were distant worlds, vast and incredibly far away, and the sun's was only one galaxy among many that sparkled in the cosmos.

But then we found out they were other galaxies! Andromeda, our neighbour, is also a rotating mass of millions of stars. Suddenly, everywhere we looked, the cosmic garden was teeming with galaxies, primary inhabitants of the universe. Eighty billion galaxies! Who knows how many more? The number kept rising the further we looked.

It had seemed that our Milky Way was part of a vast scheme with no special place and no privileged position. Suddenly, the size of the universe had leaped by a 1,000 million. Stars that could be seen with the naked eye had been vital to travellers. But telescopes had opened up cosmic continents never beheld by human eyes. The cosmos had expanded by 1,000 million and, as if that wasn't enough, by another 1,000 million. What did it all mean? There are as many stars in the sky as there are grains of sand on the seashore. What is their message?

The psalm spoke of a hillside, a young man, another millennium. A shepherd gazes at the night sky in awe, hearing within himself a voice that was not from himself. It is as if the voice said 'Write!' And David asked, 'What shall I write?' And the voice said, 'I will give you the words.' And as David looked at the vast panorama on display, illuminated by a full moon, inspiration began to flow like a river. By the light of the moon, he was able to channel that flow. Three thousand years passed. Though many pondered the beauty and immensity of the cosmos, no words ever captured so succinctly the startling position of humanity on a beautiful island in a frosty sea – or a lyrical sense of cosmic contrast. Perhaps space had seemed uninviting before. But just as frost conveyed sharp beauty and was the stuff of dreams, the heavens, though inhospitable, now shimmered with reflected power.

> When I look at your heavens, the work of your fingers,
>   the moon and the stars that you have established;
> what are human beings that you are mindful of them?
> (Psalm 8:3–4, NRSV)

During the last 5,000 orbits of the sun, generations have wondered about the cosmos. Its vastness strips away human self-importance, leaving us mute and speechless. However great the cosmos, its Maker is greater still. We look at distant worlds, still uncomprehending, then carry on our business. Yet in the face of immensity immeasurably beyond human understanding, the Bible does not tell us to collapse but praise. The secret is out. We dwell in a universe once stretched out and still growing:

> He stretches out the heavens like a canopy,
>   and spreads them out like a tent to live in.
> (Isaiah 40:22)

It was an insight reserved for our times. No one had seen it before. It cannot be all for us. Most galaxies have only recently been introduced. Immensity might reflect the age of the silent domain we inhabit: so old, so numbingly vast, uncountable galaxies flying out in all directions into the unknown. Or maybe immensity allows innumerable forms of life on any far-off planetary worlds now coming before our probing gaze. The Creator could have seeded life anywhere in the cosmos. But we have neither seen nor heard of anyone peering at us and we cannot say the universe is for us or for them. So who is it for?

Let the galaxies be a pageant of colour and sing praises. Let the endless forms and variety of stars join in witness with the marvellous range of life on earth and proclaim the creativity of the Creator, the artist who loves to walk in the garden still amid the colour and the variety of celestial objects.

What an immense sphere we behold everywhere we look at the creation. It is a theatre on the most spectacular scale for the grandeur and glory of God, the One who is supremely worthy.

Mountain peaks, rivers, lakes, waterfalls, deserts; how much the landscapes of earth have shaped the stage scenery, the setting against which the drama of human life has been played. We look up, wondering what it would be like looking down. The Creator holds the ceaseless motion of a planet. Rocks, weather and tides have a life of their own, as do we. Though dumb, they speak constantly. Mute witnesses endeavour to communicate and we pass them by. Earth is an oasis in the night. A blue and white planet with a friendly face, concealing a ceaseless inferno so the world would be alive inside and the surface replenished. There are rocky worlds and giant balls of gas that adorn the night sky. But this one was to be different. It is a planet of life. It is a globe suffused with glory, a place teeming with wonder, walked and stalked by amazing creatures.

How many are your works, O Lord!
   In wisdom you made them all;
   the earth is full of your creatures.

There is the sea, vast and spacious,
> teeming with creatures beyond number –
> living things both large and small.

(Psalm 104:24–25)

Children of the sixth day

And then there is us: children of the sixth day. 'Let us make humankind in our image' (Genesis 1:26, NRSV).

How soon humankind arose after the rest of this vast sphere of creation unfolding is for another day, another place. Suffice to say that amid battles between protagonists of the rock of ages and the ages of rocks, what can never be surrendered is that the universe had a father. It did not give rise to itself. Self-organizing systems will take us so far, but no further. In the beginning was information. Sparks that flung stars into space were lit from divine fire. God the Lord is Creator of all that can be seen and unseen. What, though, is creation? Is the act of creation a singularity – or an unfolding sequence? Does it take away from God as Creator if it be asserted creation has echoes of creative processes we see all around us – a symphony, a meal, a house, or a person? A symphony is no less an act of magisterial creation if it is a work of art that has taken time to compose. A house, or a garden, takes time for the fruition and maturity of plans. A meal is not an instant one-minute microwave job. And if at least three or four minutes, why not three or four hours of slow cooking? We have to understand creation in a way different from that of instant coffee. If an unfolding creation is not cast in the rhythm of life here on earth for a reason, why is it six days? Why not six seconds?

Every one of us begins with the mystery of a new life fused together, a foetus dividing breathtakingly, into wonder. A human child is born, the result of nine months of silent, hidden sculpturing, enacting a programme for the formation of a unique person. Skilfully, mysteriously, the hidden instructions build an arm, leg, heart, brain, skin and bones. The hidden work has taken place in each of the million children who will be born before midnight. In years to come, today will be filled with birthdays.

Are we worth anything? There's got to be more to us than these amazing bodies of ours. Two-thirds water, a pinch of salt; a brew of iodine, potassium and chemicals worth a few dollars, and then mix enough iron to make a couple of rusty nails. Is that a human being? Is that all we're worth? How did the universe come to consciousness with this absurd notion that we matter? Does the universe value the end product? How did we come up with concepts of God, physics, trust or love, or was it all the product of chemical reactions? It is said that human beings are only a set of chemicals . . . nothing but a group of neurons . . . nothing but a selfish gene . . . a number. As if everything to be said had been spoken, the mystery flushed out. Explanations reducing people to neurons, chemicals or selfish genes only left abandoned orphans bereaved of joys and sorrows, love and laughter, memories and ambitions, their identity and their freedom of choice, their purpose and their meaning.

No computer could fall in love, feel remorse or be joyful like this.

Jesus identifying with people is not joining himself to an alien race. These are people that, in due time, God personally superintended and designed. In the creation and formation of humanity, God makes something – indeed, someone – of high value. The Adam is possessed of immense value. He is made in the mirror. God's glory has entered into creation in a way that calls back to himself. That's what mirrors do. God of supreme worth and excellence sets up the world in such a way that humanity can share to some extent in that virtue and value. Thus the Adam comes to have 'value-in-oneself'.

Excursion – The mirror
The literature is vast. Due to the modern interest in what is a person, one verse has become the centre of attention, though hardly mentioned again.

> Then God said, 'Let us make humankind in our image, according to our likeness; and let them have dominion over the fish of the sea, and over the birds of the air, and over the cattle, and over all the wild animals of the earth, and over every creeping thing that creeps upon the earth.' So God created humankind in his image, in the image of God he created them; male and female he created them. (Genesis 1:26–27, NRSV)

What concerns us here is how far being made in the divine image represents a high value being placed on humanity. What would it mean to understand the creation of people as a transfer of value from God to relational, created beings made in the divine image, which call back to God at some level?

There are two elements: image (*zelem*), reflection or representation, and likeness (*demuth*). Many older writers thought that the word 'image' referred to the body, by its beauty and erectness being an expression of the divine. The idea of 'likeness' referred to our intellectual and moral nature. Augustine categorized 'image' as the rational element and 'likeness' referred to moral faculties. Scholastic theologians tended to follow this line of interpretation. Luther distinguished between 'image' and 'likeness'. The image is about our moral being, lost in the fall and recovered through redemption.[3] Reformed theologians followed Calvin in taking the middle ground between seeing the *imago* consist in rationality or in moral conformity.

Both are included.[4] Reason, conscience and will are bound up with our intellectual and moral nature, as is our capacity to know God, the foundation of our spiritual nature. 'If we were not like God, we could not know him.'[5]

Made in the mirror means that humanity possesses three Cs: consciousness, creativity and conscience.

The religious experience across the globe has witnessed countless examples of creating human (anthropomorphic) images to help devotees feel close to divine reality and that God is close to human beings. Endeavours to give form to that which is formless have been plentiful. Often, the gods were like people, reduced to finite form, allowing humans to glimpse something of the divine, or so they thought. The divine always transcends ordinary experience. It is all the more surprising that the divine can be represented by human images – people depicting his likeness, the image of God.

We are defined in relationship to God, the created representation. The creation of human beings in the image of God is not saying something has been added to the created person but is explaining what the person is. The person's very existence lives in relationship with God. Relationship with God is not something added to human existence. We are not isolated entities. The image of God does not mean that we look at ourselves as if in solitary confinement. We are hardwired for connection.

Humans are intrinsically related; it is not just in gender differentiation that we are joined at the hip. Personhood is relational. In a mirror, we see our own image. In looking at us, God sees something of himself, some recognition that leaps up, albeit in muted response. The image calls back to the image-maker in dialogue. In our horizontal relationships, there is a social refraction of our vertical connection with God. The *imago Dei* is about the value and worth of humanity. If God sees his own reflection looking back and calling back, that speaks volumes about how valuable we truly are. The image ought not to be defaced. It is a declaration of the value of personhood, but it is more than that. It is a sharing of the divine worth. Do not touch a painting or rubbish a treasured photo of someone. It represents them. A tramp is as valuable as Michelangelo because God would have it so.

God gives a vote of confidence in something he has made that resembles him in part. Humanity is a microcosm of God, gifted with the capacity to respond. Mad King George could shake hands with an oak tree, but it could not answer back. Humans might commune with nature, but not at the deep level of recognition that comes with being of like mind. It is the recognition through which a parent and child can connect. It is the recognition through which some people can remind us a little bit of God.

Time and chance

> I have seen something else under the sun:
>> The race is not to the swift
>>> or the battle to the strong,
>> nor does food come to the wise
>>> or wealth to the brilliant
>>> or favour to the learned;
>> but time and chance happen to them all.
> (Ecclesiastes 9:11)

What a mystery; a puzzle of sophistication, a knot of infinite complexity that will not be unravelled until the end of time. The divinely created sphere sings, resonant with the majesty of a knowable God; declaring the glory of an almighty instigator who made the universe knowable. Scientific methods of observation and experimentation probe the nature of reality, restlessly, ceaselessly (though science will never have the last word on reality).

Time and chance frame this vast arena in which our lives are set – inimical to human interests, or so it feels. Events happen. They just happen. Existence unfolds within a river of time; random, baffling and pointless, or so it seems. What time is, what chance is, remains the stuff of life and mystery. Things come out of nowhere and knock you down, like a car running amok on a busy high street.

The sheer contingency of life appears to run counter to any sense of humanity having awesome value. Time brings decay, though also renewal. To some, ageing comes at different rates; to all, disease and death (struck randomly by one; slain universally by the other). Without God as the meaning-maker in chief, to claim significance for humans is to hear a mocking laugh. To advance a stance of high value is to run straight into the smirk of a sphere where anything can happen. Unpredictability is predictable. Yet the laws of physics, how everything works, set things on a clear path; the stars in their courses inhabit their motion along fixed trajectory.

Such is the frame of the time-bound life. Time without change is improbable: mortality inescapable. It exists outside the mind. Time had a beginning. This all-pervasive condition of life enables us to stand outside of ourselves and compare past, present and future with heavy regret or bright-eyed anticipation. What a puzzle. As Augustine pondered, when things become past, where do they go?

Chance also poses an intellectual challenge to us of the highest order; all the more so for its also being an emotional challenge. What should be our response to life – pessimism, indifference or celebration? Much will depend on the operation of systems, the structure of forces that make and shake our world. Systems interact with systems, the weather with the economy. Yet God has a plan. Purpose and plan advance stealthily amid the nature of things. It is unlikely that all things are laid down and their courses set by mysterious divine decree. Were that so, holocaust horror would surely be banned. Somehow, God makes his way in the world. This is the arena, the landscape of life in which humanity lives, moves and has its being. The value placed on the inhabitants defies description.

Defacing the image: the trail of dishonour

God identifies with humanity and leaves something of his own being within the man and the woman, made in the divine mirror. He sets up humankind as valuable beings, beings who ought not to be rubbished. Do not degrade the little clay model of God! It is unacceptable.

The trail of dishonour began with the man and the woman accepting a seed, a thought that grew rapidly in surprisingly receptive soil. It began where affairs begin or where crime starts. 'I could do better . . .' And so the seed became a weed. Is this red-handed defiance, or humanity refusing to be bound and wanting to assert itself? On that question, the whole of human history and its theological interpretation turns. At any rate, naively stumbling into sin quickly leads to the dramatic impact. They have yielded to temptation. Self-consciousness leers at them. Truculence raises its head. 'Quick, let's hide,' they say. God, whose glory is the supreme good, has been dishonoured; worthiness devalued.

The result of not taking God seriously and turning our backs means we are facing him no longer. Devaluing God leads inexorably to the devaluing of each other, especially when we cannot cope with those who are different. This begins to play out in the genesis of things. From interpersonal acts of violence at the dawn of human life, the quest for power and control over others (a vicious cradle of life so often) becomes rooted in cultures and social systems. Evil is embedded; human devaluation reproduced, with social honour for some, social dishonour and shame for others.

Why has the church been so blind? Why so dumb? Did we have a word for it? Was it a lack of vocabulary or did we hide behind power? Perhaps when the chips were down we had no way of speaking into our cultures because we didn't realize it was our culture that spoke when we opened our lips – not God, as we naively thought. Sadly, we had misunderstood the incarnate God who embeds himself within a culture yet speaks to it – radically, dramatically.

So often the church has had an inadequate concept of sin because it did not grasp how sin is sustained and reinforced through the invisible systems that control life. If it had, it would not have condoned such evils as slavery. The haunting persistence of the dark powers is easier to spot in the inter-personal acts and the evil that men and women do. Individual sin is more obvious. Because the church over the centuries has so conspicuously failed to grasp systemic and social sin, we will return to this as a sign of the new order of things enshrined in the new humanity of Jesus.

Giving honour to humanity made in the divine mirror is intrinsic to the creative process. The *imago Dei* means that humans are made a little lower than the angels, as Psalm 8 has it. Yet the marring of that image results in humans disfiguring themselves: devaluing others and robbing God of honour. Acts and attitudes that disrespect God lead to a descending scale and stealthy collapse of human value. Descent into the heart of darkness happens through cultures and narratives that become accepted. There are five stages down. Crossing the line makes the next level conceivable:

1. **Denigration:** experiences people report of being put down, treated with indifference, sarcasm, bullying or belittling that evoke some sort of reaction.

2. **Depersonalization:** prejudice; experiences of being denied name or face, treated by impersonal economic or organizational forces as on a production line, or being written down as part of social groups neither highly prized nor standard issue. Conditioning affects result from the way society values or devalues individuals or groups on the basis of gender, class, ethnicity, disability, sexuality, age or religion. The facelessness in the systems of remote forces that control our lives erodes us.

3. **Desecration:** the essence of violence is violation. Violence is often the language of the unheard. It forcibly creates labels, shaping our sense of self. Acting in violent ways, people transmit differing messages. Respect or honour are in deficit and need to be extracted, forcibly, from the face of another. Within such blasphemous social exchange, killing someone is a sacred act.

4. **Dehumanization:** the assault on the value and dignity of persons through the indignity of human-rights abuse, human trafficking, state-sponsored violence, extreme politics or war. The focus is on the sanctity of life itself, not just loss of face and name; on political processes that either give value to the human or deny it.

5. **Demonization:** groups believing that those who are different should be denied existence are associated with a strategy of demonization. This can occur through terrorism or ethnic cleansing. Animal metaphors abound. There has never been a more sinister call than

occurred in the Rwandan genocide: 'It's time to stomp on these cockroaches!'[6] Once they call you dogs, they end up treating you worse than a dog.

Truly, the plotline of history has gained tentacles.

Election or selection?

In Old Testament narratives, the immense value given to Adam is channelled through Abraham (greatly honoured with a great future) to Israel, destined to bring universal blessing, notwithstanding their turbulent history of distress and exile. The God of all the earth? Or the God of a particular group? Where does that leave everyone else? Election works with two realities: divine call and human responsibility. How these two realities overlap is beyond our scope here (divine call is higher-order thinking). The ethnos of Israel does, though, become the means by which the universal God is expressed: partially and imperfectly. As living realities, its traditions, Scriptures and community history become the seedbed within which divine seed is to be cast into the womb of a woman.

The idea of God joining the human race for a while seems more like a hindrance than a help as we seek to engage our world more closely and make a connection. For two thousand years before God took this momentous step, he had been speaking to humanity through law and prophets. As the Old Testament amply demonstrates, God had no trouble arranging for a process of revelation whereby his mind and will could be communicated to humanity. He made contact and had not needed the incarnation to tell us about himself, as if the message had not got through before.

And then it happened.

'The incarnation opened heaven, for it was the revelation of the Word; but it also re-consecrated earth, for the Word was made flesh and dwelt among us . . . The human body itself. . . so degraded that noble minds could only view it as the enemy and prison of the soul, acquired a new meaning, exhibited new graces, and shone with a new lustre in the light of the Word made flesh.'

Charles Gore[1]

4

The humanity of God

'God joins the human race!'

Now that would make a headline, front-page news anywhere, eclipsing any social-media storm of the day.

How curious is the belief system so many contemporary people have. The message of God touching down here for a while to save the world has been discarded like an old-fashioned jacket or flared trousers no longer in fashion. But they are ready to believe in alien powers making contact. Why so swift to reject God coming to our world and becoming one of us, but so ready to believe that extraterrestrials are already here living among us? Why so quick to scorn the truth of the new day brought in by Jesus, but so ready to welcome the alien dawn? Somehow our civilization got into the position that aliens are credible but the message about Jesus is widely seen to be both incredible and irrelevant.

Having rejected God, our age is ready to embrace whatever can re-enchant the world and bring back the magic. We are the *Star Wars* generation. In Hollywood, the big hitters are stories of powers and people with powers who live outside the earth: beings that drop in on us from time to time or even dwell in disguise in our midst. They are stories of people like us in touch with cosmic power and tapping into a force that has a dark and a good side (depending on which you cultivate).

'We don't want to be alone!' we cry to the skies with a sad, empty loneliness. 'Come to us, whoever and whatever you are.' Too sophisticated to admit it, we cannot live just with ourselves. But behind us, someone is standing with out-stretched hands, someone who looks remarkably like us. If you look closely, the nail-prints are still there.

An extraordinary message was committed to the Christian church. For one brief, shining moment, God joined the human race; one with us, one of us. His sojourn was temporary. For a while he camped here, and then was gone. But the mark left where he pitched his tent will never be erased. 'And the Word became flesh and dwelt among us as in a tent, and we beheld his glory, a glory as of the only begotten of the Father, full of grace and truth' (literal Greek translation of John 1:14).

We are probing here what it means to have high value and how the church should be on the side of those who affirm it. The very idea of the incarnation of our God and Saviour as a human being supposes divine embrace – but of what? Certainly of history. Something of infinite value has entered messy history; the eternal has become time-bound. God broke through the space–time continuum to pitch his tent among us. Landscapes of history, where action and reaction jostle with memory and representation, became the divinely affirmed arena for the drama of redemption.

It is not just history in terms of the grand sweep of events that happen all around us. Jesus was possessed of a personal history, a particular individual in a particular time and space.

The historical foundation for this life is at least as strong as those for other lives. Sadly, he is neglected even in the house of his friends. For those who uphold the incarnation and defend it to the theological death are often to be found having little interest in the earthly life and self-understanding Jesus demonstrated in relation to his own mission. Except inasmuch as it validates Jesus as a divine being above all beings, and Son of God, they leap from Christmas to Easter. To all intents and purposes, the earthly history is irrelevant: a prelude to Calvary where the real business was transacted.

What exactly was it that God was affirming when he identified so personally with the human project as having immense value?

Two realities alongside each other, side by side; both are true. Humankind is used to such antinomies. Free will and determinism; light as wave and quantum particles; consciousness and brain; Jesus as fully God and fully human – there are many things, baffling but complementary. Fifth-century Christians had only metaphysics to guide theological reflection on two realities. Our times have coined new words and forged new tools, but still have little idea at what level such realities fold into each other. At least we are beyond the systematizing reflex of modernity. Neuroscience is our latest tool. The idea of the soul, both immortal and immaterial, has not fared well with a consensus in cognitive science that all mental and spiritual life is rooted in neural activity. Maybe a return to monism means going back to Hebrew roots rather than Greek dualism. Our true selfhood is not some immaterial essence incarcerated in this ageing shell. The soul is God-breathed life.

It is beyond our scope here to probe the difficult journey by which our theological forefathers sought to affirm that Christ the Saviour is one and is therefore able to unite humankind with God. Did Jesus have a rational human soul

or did the divine Logos replace it? Could Jesus, as the embodiment of the divine–human union, comprehend sin in a truly
human way? Where was the partition? Or was it, as in one
celebrated analogy, akin to a drop of vinegar (the human
dimension) being swallowed up by an ocean of divine life? In
this life, our sense of ourselves is rooted in the flesh. We experience incarnation through the developing journey of the body
through time. The Son of God had embraced the capacity for
human thoughts, human desires and freedom. Human ways
of experiencing and knowing were now open to him. There
are after all two different ways of cognition. The human mind
knows things gradually, by experiment, by experience. Divine
mind knows things intuitively, directly and eternally. The
divine mind had access to the human mind but not vice versa.

The incarnation gives meaning and purpose to the physical
unity of being human. It is a great and noble thing to be
human. It must be so for God has endorsed it through identification and solidarity. God's entry into our humanity
represents the greatest possible affirmation and elevation of
the human. Irenaeus, second-century theologian and Bishop
of Lyons, wrote words that are routinely hijacked by CEOs in
management self-help: 'The glory of God is a human being
fully alive!' The glory of God is humanity 'alive'. Actually, he
said no such thing. 'Life in man is the glory of God; the life
of man is the vision of God,' is what he wrote.[2] This is the
beatific vision; seeing God as the essence of human life rather
than a humanist vision devoid of divinity.

Our times run into the intellectual quagmire debating what
it means to be fully human or to be a self. Values, ethical
frameworks, genetic engineering or gender reassignment
combine with the new empire of neuroscience to create a
miasma of meaning. Technology, the internet and artificial
intelligence constantly push the boundaries of what is the

point of being human when our lives are lived more and more in cyberspace. The rise of the robots either enhances or threatens us all.

It is all very well saying that the incarnation of the divine Word was by definition a vote in favour of embodiment. The body is a building site now. Healthiness, obesity, sexuality, body image – to name but a few arenas of battle – mean that the body is a central concern in social science, not just physiology. What 'the body' means is now up in the air.

As Clement of Alexandria argued in the last decade of the pivotal second century, the image of God is the ground of the mystic union believers can have with Christ. All truth and goodness, wherever it is found, comes from the one who made us. Clement strongly opposed Gnostics who looked down with disdain on the created order and especially the human body. Matter is not alien substance. Sex is not incompatible with being spiritual. The body is not lower or second class. Jesus valued bodily life.

It is curious that in our time the very idea of incarnation is anathema to many sophisticates. Our vagabond age can salute reincarnation, but incarnation is outside of the general world view of thinking people and the unthinking alike – apart from ghosts of Christmas past stalking the corridors of memory and imagination. It is we who shake and rattle our chains in response.

Down or up?

There have been two main routes through which to approach the most immense and influential person in human history. The first is to probe an apparently simple question – how did Jesus become God? How did a first-century Jewish teacher come to be regarded as on a par with God?

Somehow, the divine Lord of humanity came to be seen as having taken the initiative and come to our level. As an old man, Simeon, grasped that morning in Jerusalem, God has finally come to us.

This route starts with making some very human assumptions about Jesus as a mysterious yet very human figure who possessed such remarkable presence and power, and influenced so many, that he was elevated beyond his contemporaries and accorded divine status. Somehow, Jesus came to be given an unprecedented identity and position. Christianity is about him. Such was his impact that he came to be seen as revealing God in a unique way: a mirror of God. Jesus was human, it is argued, but his humanity became *a* very full demonstration of God, not *the* definitive and unique one.

The contemporaries of Jesus came initially by this pathway. For his immediate followers and even in such a staunchly monotheistic climate, Jesus came to be regarded as a man yet more than a man. What was it they were encountering that pushed their grasp of God and humanity? Rather than beating their brains trying to figure it out, gradually they responded to it. The teaching of Jesus, his character and especially the power that was at work through him, was beyond anything they had known. It came to a head at Caesarea Philippi, from which the Jordan sets out on its southward track, the spot where statues of the gods were placed. In a twilight, murky world, where gods became human and humans became gods by promotion, came the probing question: 'What are the people saying about me? Who do you say that I am?' Peter gave voice to an instinctive grasp: 'You are the Christ' (Mark 8:29).

Shortly afterwards in Mark's account, from the mount of transfiguration, it was downhill all the way. Down there lay the inexorable cross, the valley of humiliation and vale of tears. Conceptions lay torn asunder until, from tattered fragments and human wreckage, a new perception arose on the third day: 'through the Spirit of holiness [Jesus] was declared with power to be the Son of God by his resurrection from the dead' (Romans 1:4).

Such was the stumbling, slow realization of the contemporaries of the Christ. For others who never did find their way up the summit, the situation was radically different. Invoking deep traditions in their history and prophecy, Jesus threw down the gauntlet. The kingdom of God was on the march. Renewing the covenant, God would come again to his people. The return of the King would be the decisive moment, the beginning of the end and the end of the beginning. Temple theology would no longer protect them. Jesus was challenging the whole religious power base – and Caiaphas knew it.

But the times were a-changin'. It is this sense of vocation and unique role in bringing in the kingdom of God that characterized the self-understanding that Jesus seems to have had. Consciousness of being the second person of the Trinity and the eternal Son is not a way of thinking that is conspicuous in Matthew, Mark or Luke (with the exception of a text like Matthew 11:27). What we do have is teaching acted out, true drama involving unique speech acts. Yet like any applicant for a role these days, there is not just a job description but a person specification. Who is it who can fill these shoes? What kind of person was needed to undertake the inauguration of a new age through restoring God to his rightful place? More importantly, what kind of person was it who embodied the dramatic and totally unexpected witness to the resurrection that validated such a total reversal?

The other main route has been to approach the question of Jesus, not just via another path to the summit but from the summit itself going downward. This hails the one-off incarnation of our God and Saviour Jesus Christ. Jesus 'from above' is the call to be faithful to the biblical message about descent. God has joined himself to our humanity and become one of us while remaining fully God.

The word is 'kenosis', the self-emptying of Jesus to be receptive to the will of the Father, the one who made himself nothing. '[He] emptied himself' (Philippians 2:7, NRSV). The stoop of God in embracing the human situation is the model for Christians to divest themselves of self-interested power and respond with joyful imitation. It is not so much a theory as a call to arms – or a call to be harmless. It is not what the Son gave up, but what he gained. It is not the royal status he left, but the servant role he embraced in comprehensive self-restraint.

Of what did Christ empty himself? This was a vital question when the debate about whether Jesus was fully divine rent the fourth-century church. 'Kenotic theory', a joyless phrase, strips away the divinity from the Word made flesh. The nineteenth-century Lutheran Gottfried Thomasius suggested that Jesus divested himself of the God-attributes such as omniscience, omnipresence and omnipotence. Christ weakened himself voluntarily so that he could function as a human being to accomplish something powerful: the work of human redemption. It still assumes the pre-existence of Christ: that he had lived before (though not as a human). Philippians has nothing to say about the God-attributes, though. It is about power; the imitation and the limitation, the humility that moved him to seek a far lesser status. To be sure, Jesus accepted limitations. Biblical Christianity has urged that he voluntarily accepted self-imposed limits. Its witness has been that Jesus remained fully divine while so doing, thus enabling human redemption to take place. Living in union with God, Jesus gave up none of his divine attributes. He gave up not some part of himself but status.

Kenosis has fewer friends today. It has become more fashionable now to say that the self-emptying took place in Jesus' own experience while he was alive, or at the cross as he embraced the Father's will. In the days of his flesh, there was then a repeated emptying of himself. Jesus had powers upon which he could have called to deliver himself, but he refused to use them. He had knowledge he could have deployed, but refused to use it. Jesus did not know quantum physics.

In attempting to define what it was he left behind and how he then functioned, thinkers are dealing with something without parallel. In Jesus, we do not encounter someone else, we touch God directly; we touch God personally. Non-trinitarian groups would deny this and say that Jesus was god with a small 'g', an ambassador of divinity, a representative. They have cut the essential link that makes Jesus an embodiment of God on earth. But that is not mainstream Christian teaching. The coming of the divine being into the world as a human being cannot be about how much divinity can be shrunk into humanity and still retain one or the other. Neither can it be acceptable to say that we are just as much an incarnation of God as Jesus was; certainly not functioning as a Spirit-anointed servant on the same terms as all who would follow. The incarnation of God in human form was not one of a kind but a one-off, unique event in our world.

Christ embraced our situation in full. But what does it mean for one person to be a representative of humanity given that humanness is very particular in time and place? Here we have a first-century Jewish male standing in solidarity with the experience of common humanity from the inside.

Does it matter if it was God in person who came among us or whether it was someone else who was sent? Yes it does. Jesus was either a living, walking, talking embodiment of God or God sent a third party to be his representative. In Jesus, we are not touching a third party. We are encountering God directly, authentically, not merely his ambassador. This was a totally unique individual in world history who did not just have more of God in him than anyone else, but was someone who could truly say, 'Anyone who has seen me has seen the Father' (John 14:9).

In this post-millennial era, can we still believe that God comes down here in person? Surely God is within us all already, all around us and upholding everything that breathes and moves? The idea of God inserting himself into the folds of human history raises profound philosophical issues.

A generation ago, the earth was supposed to have moved when Bishop John Robinson wrote his controversial 1963 bestseller *Honest to God*. It claimed to have knocked down the old idea of God up there as an old man in the sky whom we could no longer believe in. Bishop Robinson said, and presumably he should know, that God was not up there but maybe inside us or around us, the ground of our being and of all life itself – what they call 'immanence'.

Of course he was knocking down a straw caricature of what Christians have believed about God. Some people no doubt saw God as living up there beyond the clouds wearing a beard. But most Christians were sensible enough to realize that this was a figure of speech; that God was beyond ourselves, greater than ourselves, but also separate from his creation. Talk about God is not just another way of talking about the universe. God is free to speak and act in his creation. He is greater than the cosmos. The universe is not the sum total of God or a part of God. In Jesus, God the transcendent sovereign Creator of the universe came down to our level. Jesus is Emmanuel, God with us, one of us. He is not a remote figure. God is not a transcendent being who runs the whole cosmos but stays aloof from a messy human life.

'Tell us what God is like. We want to reach out and make contact with the ultimate power.' This summarizes the religious and spiritual quest of humanity.

God has come to us, reached out and taken human form in a way that we can recognize and handle. If he had come as an alien being of mind-blowing power, we could not relate to him. But God came to our world once in a form we can recognize and get to grips with. The invisible God became visible, the immaterial has materialized so we can see and relate to him. The Lord of all, who towers above and beyond us in every conceivable way, has taken recognizable shape and shrunk to our size. The God of glory divested himself of his majesty and put on the tattered robes of our humanity.

Jesus is indeed the real article, the genuine expression of God on earth. Through Jesus we discover what God thinks, what God feels about things, what God is like and what God likes, the compassion of God and what makes him angry. This was not a book or an angel being dispatched with a message to the people of earth. Jesus represents God himself coming to us to be one of us and get involved with us.

Theological affirmations and creeds assume 'descent'. The beyond has come near. Jesus is the one who came down so as to get on to our level. For the first Christians or his contemporaries, Jesus was completely baffling, breaking down the categories about what people do or humans say. After his resurrection, those who claimed to have seen the risen Lord clustered together to follow Christ.

The early church moved in the direction of travel that came to a destination at a place called Chalcedon. Now a district of Istanbul, then it was an ancient maritime town of Bithynia. Between 8 October and 1 November AD 451, Chalcedon witnessed an ecumenical gathering. The council declared that Jesus was perfect in Godhead and also perfect in manhood, truly God and truly human. It rejected the idea that Jesus had a single nature. Rather there were two realities side by side; divine and human alongside each other. There were, to be sure, some difficult terms to fathom. What is 'person', 'nature' and the mysterious word 'hypostasis'? Theologians found they were dealing with what it means to be a person, not just a God-person but personhood of any sort.

'The Word became flesh.' He assumed human nature. It is not what God gave up but what he added, what he took on. The great addition was that this was God taking humanity to himself. As Leo the Great said, 'Who was true God was born, complete in his own nature, complete in ours.'[3]

The nationalized industries of truth

If we really do believe that God once joined the human race, then it raises all the issues of intolerance and exclusivism. It would be easier were Christian thinking not wedded to the idea of God becoming embodied in a carpenter from Nazareth. Perhaps we should quietly drop this claim and emphasize Christian values instead? Late-modern people object profoundly to a one-off act of identification. 'Surely God could have become embodied many times. Why do you Christians say that only one man, Jesus, is the authorized version of God?' It seems exclusive and intolerant.

But our message about the uniqueness of Jesus really is that there has been a definitive, genuine expression of God. To save the world, the Creator became a human being once and once only. It would indeed be much easier if we could say that this remarkable act of identification has taken place several times, that gurus and avatars were also an embodiment of God, or that Jesus is one of many. There would be far more points of contact with the millions interested in fuzzy spirituality if

God did indeed dwell in us all and that one figure is not an exclusive guide on the pathway.

We dwell in a marketplace of ideas, a pluralist society governed by market forces and consumer demand. Every idea is valid and to suggest otherwise brings a frown. The great sin of the day is intolerance. Any claim to have the sole truth is an affront to be referred to the spiritual equivalent of the anti-trust commission. No one must be called wrong. Yet today the nationalized industries of truth are broken up. In our spirituality, we are all capitalists now. No longer will we wear any concept of authority, for we wear a different robe. No-one will tell us what to do, what to believe or how to live our lives. In our morality, we are anarchists. Oligarchy is out, democracy is in, and long live freedom of choice! 'In those days, Israel had no king; everyone did as he saw fit' (Judges 21:25).

But even though at one stroke it would remove a stumbling block to marketing the good news if Christians did not seem to have a spiritual monopoly, there are powerful reasons why we cannot surrender the uniqueness of God's identification with humanity in Christ.

The idea of someone becoming a revelation of God on earth is not unique to Christianity. But the identification of God with humanity as Jesus is light years away from the world of avatars and gurus. Christianity is not a human trying to achieve God-realization but God achieving human-realization. Do other faiths claim that God has personally identified with the world? Maybe the embodiment of God on earth could have been revealed in India, central Africa or Manhattan – not once but several times. Maybe Jesus could have been born in Manchester, rather than simply expressing himself through people. He or she has yet to be born who did not have a gap in the soul, a yearning stretching towards the ultimate power behind every-thing. But there the similarity ends. The incarnation is unique.

Every religion and every philosophy is humankind reaching out to the ultimate power behind everything to make contact and resolve the contradictions of our human existence, the sinfulness and the pain – every faith except for one. Christianity has a distinct calling card. It is God visiting humanity, coming down to our level, identifying with us.

For thirty years there was a hidden seed growing that burst into the open and then flowered for three years. During those thirty years, the world was oblivious to the secret identity. Then Jesus began to make himself known, not by a great new conference or pronouncement but inductively, deductively, until the seed had taken in sufficient numbers of other people to be alive in the world.

The significance of Jesus being God's Son first began to grow on soil that was completely unfavourable. We have lost sight of how astonishing that was. As in India today, in the Greek world of thought the idea of gods revealing themselves in human form was fairly commonplace. The old gods of Olympus regularly took human form and were seen as people like us. The nature-god Pan assumed human form (as any reader of *The Wind in the Willows* will recall). Alexander the Great was a divine man, the son of the gods. And the Roman world was busy working on the more recent memory of Caesar, elevating his legend into the rank of the gods. In those countries and that climate of ideas, people thought gods did indeed come down to us. Gods became men and men became gods. It did not take much to provoke a claim to incarnation. 'When the crowd saw what Paul had done, they shouted in the Lycaonian language, "The gods have come down to us in human form!" Barnabas they called Zeus, and Paul they called Hermes because he was the chief speaker' (Acts 14:11–12).

The message about Jesus had to take root in an area where there were fierce antibodies in the bloodstream to anything other than monotheism. Maybe it would have been easier if Jesus had been incarnated in another country, another world of thought. This very resistance in ancient Israel to God dropping in on us makes the message about Jesus all the more remarkable. The fact that the act of divine identification took place in ancient Israel shows why it was a one-off event. Jesus arrived in a context, a tradition. It was a line of expectation and build-up that gave the right setting for the embodiment of God, rooted in a particular place at a particular time, in a culture disposed to anticipating God's kingdom. Matthew places Jesus in a long line of preparation. 'All this took place to fulfil what the Lord had said through the prophet: "The virgin will be with child and will give birth to a son, and they will call him Immanuel" – which means, "God with us"' (Matthew 1:22–23).

'The virgin shall be with child'? Virgin birth seems an antiquated idea but is definitely a misnomer. His birth was as normal as anyone's: his conception is what remains controversial. Many argue that the statement in the earliest Christian writing, 'God sent his son, born of a woman' (Galatians 4:4), does not have to imply supernatural conception in a way that is radically different from that of anyone else. Massive wisdom and cogency as such proponents possess, the conundrum remains nonetheless. How does Jesus avoid being like anyone else (albeit brimming over with divinity) unless God is directly involved such as has not happened before or since in the annals of human reproduction? Say that this is not God inserting himself into the folds of humanity and immediately you are saying that this is a man full of God but not God in person. The game-changer has changed. The circumstances of his coming were unrepeatable by definition. He was born into a tradition, into the story of God with his world. He was not born in Manchester.

5

Becoming human (the manual)

We only grasp why the good news is good news when we see how the life and death of Jesus connects with our humanity. The death of Christ only intersects with human experience so powerfully because his entire life did so – immeasurably and profoundly.

How real is your Christ? The humanity of Jesus is only an issue because we want to say divine things about him. Being faithful to the biblical witness requires us to affirm that it was God who became human rather than a human being who became God. The question that has dogged Christian thought is how this double reality can be so stated that one part of it does not prevail at the expense of the other.

Probably the very first heresy the church had to confront was Docetism – from the Greek word *dokein*, to seem. The church was obliged to combat the false Gnostic teaching that Jesus had only appeared to be human and was God in disguise. This did not constitute identification whereby Jesus affirmed the value and worth of human physicality. The Hebrews letter and other New Testament texts affirmed what was being preached about Jesus, that he had lived before and came to the world, a pre-existent figure on a divine rescue mission for humanity. In medieval pictures, Jesus is portrayed as an unreal, ghostly figure, to be identified by the halo that surrounded him. It was against these docetic tendencies that Martin Luther made one of his great contributions to the person of Jesus. To understand him properly, we must begin from below; after that, come upwards. Start with the truth of his humanity and work from there to affirm the truth of the deity of Jesus.[1]

This was after all the route by which the disciples began to realize the identity of Jesus. Genuineness in his humanity was never questioned, but they were compelled to take in the reality of what they encountered, which is accessible to us too – a reality that led them to conclude that Jesus was a man but somehow more than a man. The more that 'the God in him' came to be understood and Jesus began to be seen as a pre-existent being who had come from heaven, then the more the authenticity of his humanity was open to question. How could they have it both ways, they reasoned?

His humanity was real and genuine. Jesus was genuinely God and genuinely human – at the same time. There are powerful reasons for insisting on the total solidarity of Jesus 'with us' and 'for our salvation'. Jesus is God for us because he is the person for others, the one for all, a representative human being. Jesus stood in solidarity with all humanity, not just those who happened to be a Jewish male under oppressive occupation. Jesus is the representative person for all social locations, whether, for example, the experiences of Afghan women or those with disability.

What Jesus did acquire and embrace were insider experiences. Theologically, his solidarity is best approached through a resonance whereby the human experiences he subjected himself to were those common to all. What conditions did Jesus accept as one of us?

Excursion – The long silence (an anonymous story)

At the end of time, billions of people were seated on a great plain before God's throne. Most shrank back from the brilliant light before them. But some groups near the front talked heatedly, not cringing with cringing shame, but with belligerence.

'Can God judge us? How can he know about suffering?' snapped a young woman. She ripped open a sleeve to reveal a tattooed number from a Nazi concentration camp. 'We endured terror . . . beatings . . . torture . . . death!'

In another group a young man lowered his collar. 'What about this?' he demanded, showing an ugly rope burn. 'Lynched, for no crime but being black!'

In another crowd there was a pregnant schoolgirl with sullen eyes: 'Why should I suffer?' she murmured. 'It wasn't my fault.'

Far out across the plain were hundreds of such groups. Each had a complaint against God for the evil and suffering he had permitted in his world.

How lucky God was to live in heaven, where all was sweetness and light. Where there was no weeping or fear, no hunger or hatred. What did God know of all that human beings had been forced to endure in this world? For God leads a pretty sheltered life, they said.

So each of these groups sent forth their leader, chosen because he or she had suffered the most: a Jew, a black person, someone from Hiroshima, a person disabled by chronic arthritis, a thalidomide child. In the centre of the vast plain, they consulted with each other. At last they were ready to present their case. It was rather clever.

Before God could be qualified to be their judge, he must endure what they had endured. Their decision was that God should be sentenced to live on earth as a man.

Let him be born a Jew. Let the legitimacy of his birth be doubted. Give him a work so difficult that even his family will think him out of his mind.

Let him be betrayed by his closest friends. Let him face false charges, be tried by a prejudiced jury and convicted by a cowardly judge. Let him be tortured.

At the last, let him see what it means to be terribly alone. Then let him die so there can be no doubt he died. Let there be a great host of witnesses to verify it.

As each leader announced his or her portion of the sentence, loud murmurs of approval went up from the throng of people assembled. When the last had finished pronouncing sentence, there was a long silence. No one uttered a word. No one moved.

For, suddenly, all knew that God had already served his sentence.

'A difficult start in life'

Jesus certainly experienced a great deal of life – raw, rugged life. For a start, he was a member of a race that has attracted more hostility than any throughout history. Jesus was **born Jewish**.

The politics of hate whipped up by Nazi mythology was the worst and most recent manifestation of a spiritual cancer that has rotted Western civilization for centuries. It is baffling why the Jews have drawn down such odium and occasioned such hatred. Even the term 'Jew' has been one of abuse that has filled whole societies with fear and loathing. Mention 'Zionists' at the United Nations and stand back! When the Romans determined to destroy the rebellion in Israel, they ran out of trees on which to crucify the Jewish people. Yet it was this hated race that Jesus joined and God identified with. And he became the symbolic Jewish sufferer, experiencing the personal holocaust that falls to the servant of the Lord (Isaiah 53).

Jesus had to endure the slur of **illegitimacy** that dogged him through his life. It was his constant companion. ' "We are not illegitimate children," they protested. "The only Father we have is God himself" ' (John 8:41). People through all ages have known what that is like. The slander, the whispering, the second-class treatment, the love child who must be kept hidden, rape's result, the single or divorced mum struggling against the social stigma – Jesus experienced it too. The pressures and the words that relegate human beings were his chosen lot amid the chosen people.

The circumstances of his birth show **bureaucracy** at work. 'Everyone went to his own town to register' (Luke 2:3) – words that roll off the Christmas story with hardly a thought. But what an inconvenience for Joseph and Mary! Imagine that the baby is growing inside her. And then the news comes that everyone is to return to the town of their birth to register. The prospective parents must have hoped that, given those circumstances, the timing would still work out for them, that they could travel the ninety miles or so down to Bethlehem with the baby already born or at least be back just in time for the birth. It must have been with a heavy heart that they had to face the unavoidable, and a heavily pregnant Mary left with Joseph. The ordeal must have seemed to them the result of bureaucracy, as though they were victims of a decree made in the equivalent of Brussels or Washington.

With all who have known the impact of regimented regulations that will brook no exceptions, Jesus stands in solidarity. For all who have been told, 'Those are the rules,' or been rounded up to become a number, a statistic, we have news.

Jesus has become one of us. After all, what difference did it make for the Roman Empire to have overlooked Joseph and Mary under the circumstances? A few numbers here and there. 'They can't be serious, they can't expect us to do this . . . Don't they know how inconvenient this is? I'm a name, not a number!' God himself has been there and done that.

As a baby, Jesus experienced **homelessness**. 'She wrapped him in cloths and placed him in a manger, because there was no room for them in the inn' (Luke 2:7). Let's remind ourselves what mangers are. The Son of God opted not for a birth in a king's palace with soft conditions, linen and warmth. He opted for an animal feeding trough. What a rude awakening into the world! But no child in a slum need think his Lord chose a comfier place than him and asked for special privileges. Then, as now, there was no room for the homeless, and Jesus shared those experiences too. Amid their burst of praise that night, the angels might have grasped what would not be understood for a time, that God identified with all people, not just the rich and famous. A motley group of night workers, a Jewish peasant girl, a stable for a birth – these are images not of wealth and power but raw images accessible to everyone. Prophetically, Mary herself saw what was going on:

> he has scattered those who are proud in their
>   inmost thoughts.
> He has brought down rulers from their thrones
>   but has lifted up the humble.
> He has filled the hungry with good things
>   but has sent the rich away empty.
> (Luke 1:51–53)

Homeless people the world over can know that God opted to join their situation when he became embodied as a human being. The effect of the temperature dropping in a Ukrainian winter is to send orphan children scurrying into the sewers in search of warmth. Many of them do not have shoes. Or think of the 150 million street kids of Brazil or Columbia or 150 other places. Or the 600 who sleep rough in London on any one night – among them a 19-year-old young woman I knew of who had bird-like arms marked by the heroine she had injected. For all those whose identity is that of being a homeless person, Jesus joined their insecure ranks.

Jesus also identified with **disease**. A modern public health official would have boiled over at a baby being born in a stable. A Bethlehem choked with visitors would have been a natural breeding ground for a wide variety of diseases and infections. Insanitary, overcrowded conditions were an ideal medium. And a stable was suited to the spread of diseases that human beings catch from animals. Gut-borne bacteria like E. coli, salmonella, tetanus were all hazards. If the stable was home to sheep and cows, there was the additional risk of brucellosis (from cows) as well as orf (a pox transmitted by sheep). All in all, it was a miracle that the newborn child survived under those conditions.

Jesus would have experienced surely the anxiety and **trauma** of sudden flight. Imagine the circumstances. Joseph is warned in a dream to escape. He says to Mary with alarm, 'We have to get out, now!' After all, Bethlehem was only a short distance from Jerusalem. It wouldn't have taken long for the soldiers to get there. There would inevitably have been an atmosphere of worry and panic that would have been communicated to the young child. Children absorb atmospheres like that even if they can't articulate it. Not that Jesus would be emotionally scarred by the experience. But he stands in solidarity with all those who have experienced sudden panic or terror on the day when the soldiers came. Matthew, who records these things, goes on to toll the bell for the death of the children. Joseph and Mary knew what they had escaped from and made it known to Jesus.

Then Jesus moves around and experiences life in another culture. His first five years were spent in Egypt. That too would have an effect. I think of missionary children or sons and daughters of modern executives, who moved to other cultures in their childhood. Jesus identifies with them all.

Asylum seekers too can realize that here is a saviour for them. Nobody wants to be made homeless or become an asylum seeker. That should evoke compassion, care and welcome from the church that follows Jesus Christ. Today there are more than 22 million refugees, three-quarters of them women and children. But though many of them are too traumatized even to tell their story, the story of a God who got involved intersects with their lives and offers hope, freedom and security. Maybe the empathy of God demonstrated through his church starts with recognition of how we would feel were we in their shoeless feet, desperate for understanding and practical help.

The child next door

Back in Nazareth, Jesus would have gone to school. From earliest days, every Jewish child was instructed at home and taught religious customs and the Torah. In one of the tractates of the Talmud, it was said to be unlawful to live in a place where there was no school. It was probably in the synagogue at Nazareth, maybe under the tuition of the rabbi, that Jesus was taught to read and write using the text of Torah. When he was ten, Jesus would have gone on to study traditional law, the Mishna, afterwards to theological discussion of the Talmud. It is a narrow syllabus to modern ears and there was little geometry, mathematics, science, history or geography in the curriculum.

In his humanity Jesus had an enquiring mind and learned quickly. An incident when he was twelve demonstrates this, and it is the only time the curtain is drawn back during the hidden years. The boy in the temple astounds the rabbis at Jerusalem with how much he knew and by the sharpness of his insight (Luke 2:46). So Jesus experienced education. He had to go through all that too.

Whether he would have got all the answers right is another matter. To be human, Jesus was surely capable of error. This raises the fascinating question of how much Jesus knew in himself. Did Jesus understand quantum physics? As God, the answer is yes. He invented quantum physics. Here we come to the limitation that Jesus experienced in his incarnation. As the eternal Logos, the pre-existent Son, he expressed the very mind of God. As a human being, there had to be a considerable limiting of what was possible if he was to be genuinely human. To put it mildly, if he had kept track of what was going on in distant galaxies all the while he was a human being, it would have blown the circuits. Families often move from a larger house to a smaller one. It is not easy to shrink and condense yourself, especially after accumulating so much. Imagine moving from palace to garden shed. God has condensed himself, so to speak, shrunk to the size of humanity. Theologians call it kenosis, God emptying himself. As a human being, Jesus probably did not know quantum physics.

The hidden years of Nazareth represent a time of full-blown identification with the routines of life. Jesus learnt a trade. Although 'carpenter' may be a label rather than job description, he certainly learnt how life is put together in a world other than just spiritual. He had to find out how the world works and what makes people tick. His parables show acute observation of life and situations that Jesus probably did not invent on the spot but had spun out of everyday life, woven from what he encountered first hand.

In those years of learning and growing, Jesus knew what it was to build a life, to get up in the morning and go to work. For all those who experience the drudgery of life and have to knuckle down on Monday mornings, Jesus has been there too. God has identified himself with working people and redeemed the workplace. For many people, it remains the case that work is not a spiritual occupation compared with being a missionary. The incarnation of Jesus should shatter any illusions that Christianity isn't about work and compel us to connect with this vital part of the human situation.

Jesus experienced relative poverty. He accepted the conditions of a working man of his time, grinding out the work that had to be done, or there would be no bread on the table. Jesus knew the struggle to make ends meet and the uncertainty of business demand. God accepted that he would be placed in a situation of struggle, not of idleness or ease or luxury. We would love to know how many rooms they had in the family home. It couldn't have been very spacious. Jesus is not depicted as a beggar. But he did have to work for a living.

He knew what it was to be subject to parents: 'He went down to Nazareth with them and was obedient to them' (Luke 2:51). Was Jesus smacked for getting into mischief? We recoil from questions like this because our hymns about the incarnation say that all good Christians should be 'mild, obedient, good as he'. But the fact that many people get a reaction from singing that line highlights our confusion. We know that Christian children get up to mischief. So can Christian adults. Surely Jesus was no angel. He identified himself with children and parents, an ordinary, messy family life, and the process of continual negotiation that goes with the territory. Maybe he lived alone for a while and might have yearned in his twenties for independence and to set up home for himself.

Jesus experienced the messiness of ordinary family life. He had brothers and sisters (Mark 3:32). Again, here is an area where the Christian church has wanted to protect the deity of Jesus. Roman Catholics have often taught that Mary and Joseph did not have sexual relations after Jesus was born – and definitely not before. They were trying to keep Jesus special, but this is an unnecessary way of doing it. His was a robust humanity and did not need to be put in a glass jar. Neither did Mary need to be protected against the later idea that sex transmitted original sin. If the church had taken the identification principle seriously, it would never have got into such teaching. The incarnation affirmed the life of the body.

Jesus was no hermit. John the Baptist lived in the desert until his public ministry began (Luke 1:80). But Jesus has redeemed family life. Why a movement should begin in the third century espousing that monasticism and solitary Christianity was a superior path to holiness is difficult to see. Maybe they were following in the footsteps of John the Baptist rather than the One who identified with family life and embraced it.

But this also tells us that Jesus knew what it was to look after ageing parents and to go through life in all its cycles. They looked after him. Now in his earthly life, he will fulfil all his obligations and responsibilities. He never said, 'I'm a preacher, I'm above all that.' He had learnt how to live a natural life, invested with the quality of God. No-one ever slandered his character. Jesus would have been a reliable, faithful man of good reputation in the community, known for honesty and patience.

Jesus experienced **bereavement**. At some point, Jesus stood with his father's coffin. Did he go through these experiences unscathed? They must have helped to shape him. If his incarnation is for real, in his identification with humanity, God and humanity meet – and God is changed by the encounter (not God as he is in himself, but God as the unique combination of divine and human). But Jesus knew the gut-wrenching sense of emptiness and sadness that comes with bereavement, the amputation of what has been a part of us, the sense of loss at the permanent emigration of a loved one, the sudden responsibility laid upon his shoulder. The heart of bereavement is the pain of letting go. Jesus himself has been there. Jesus did not want to sail through life unharmed. He embraced personal pain. For all those who have experienced bereavement, we have good news. Jesus has identified himself with us and can fill every hole. 'We do not have a high priest who is unable to sympathise with our weaknesses, but we have one who has been tempted in every way, just as we are – yet was without sin' (Hebrews 4:15).

The sixty-four-thousand-dollar question is, 'What about love and sex?' There are enormous barriers in our minds to people even asking that question, whether Jesus is one of us with sexual desires. Was Jesus a normal human being if he was without sexuality? But surely, if God has really identified with humanity, that extends to desire and the cry for intimacy that is so much a part of us.

After all, love and sex are so fundamental to what it means to be human, the highs and the lows, the triumph and the tragedy, the glory and the shame. If we automatically suppose that Jesus was incapable of entering into the longing, the agony and the ecstasy, was it really a human life we saw?

In choosing celibacy, Jesus redeemed singleness. If Jesus yielded to the physical expression of that, he would not be the man for others, who must commit himself to humanity, not just one person. If the richest life that has ever been lived was single and fulfilled, that is good news for all. Jesus was so alive, so full of a positive overflowing attitude that he could give it away. 'I have come that they may have life, and have it to the full' (John 10:10). A morose, incomplete man could not have said that.

Jesus had to do something with the cry for intimacy, and he had a unique and close relationship with the Father that was deeply part of his being (not an optional extra). But Jesus also invested himself richly in his friendships. It is only reasonable to suppose that Jesus had many friends while he was growing up. During his ministry, his disciples were his friends. That's why the earliest Christianity is wealthy in talk of fellowship. 'Therefore, my brothers and sisters, whom I love and long for, my joy and crown, stand firm in the Lord in this way, my beloved' (Philippians 4:1, NRSV).

This was rather different from the pattern of hierarchy and authority that was to characterize the Christian church subsequently. Here is a fellowship. It was both an impetus and a style of Christian leadership that went back to Jesus: 'You are my friends if you do what I command' (John 15:14); 'Could you men not keep watch with me for one hour?' (Matthew 26:40). Peter was not just his protégé and John not just on a training course. They were friends. Jesus was known for his friends. He even had close friendships with women (Luke 8:1–2). Whether Mary Magdalene and Mary of Bethany might have been one and the same, there is a pattern of deep friendship unheard of for a rabbi.

At the home of Mary and Martha, a dinner was given in Jesus' honour. Lazarus was there, in the best of health but possibly quiet after his recent experience. Martha served, doing what she was most comfortable doing. And Mary of Bethany took a whole pint of perfume and anointed Jesus for burial (a year's wages was too cheap a present). There is in this scene an atmosphere of friendship. Women had watched him dying, and now on resurrection morning, Mary is going to anoint his body. But then we have the tender scene in the garden when Jesus stands before her though she is blinded with tears. 'Mary,' he says, and she gasps with astonishment and rapidly changing emotions as when the sun dispels the shadow. 'Rabboni!' Jesus replies. 'Do not hold on to me, for I have not yet returned to the Father. Go instead to my brothers . . .' (John 20:16–17). This is friendship at its tenderest. The Christian church would have been a very different kind of place if the atmosphere of friendship had remained. (There is still hope.)

Jesus certainly experienced physical **hunger**. There may have been times of hardship in the family home when the next meal was a question mark. Jesus was born into relative poverty, and reduced harvests would have affected him like anybody else in the village. He did not choose to have a charmed life. It is likely that, on their campaigns, food and money may have been tight at times, though Judas was as efficient a treasurer as you can get. The band of disciples would have to depend on what they were given.

Hunger definitely knocked at his door when he fasted for forty days. 'Knocked at his door' is an understatement – it would have been a loud din of a thumping, not a gentle tapping. But then so is the phrase in Luke's Gospel: 'He ate nothing during those days, and at the end of them he was hungry' (Luke 4:2). This understatement does show the self-mastery that Jesus had. But the reality of hunger was there, and Jesus did not shrink from experiencing it. Neither did he carve out a definition of humanity that excluded the sharpness of hunger pangs.

For thirty years, Jesus lived a normal life in a village, in a nation under foreign occupation. Growing up in Nazareth would have been a very different experience from growing up in Western Samoa or Manchester. Jesus lived life in the real world before embarking on his ministry.

A representative life

His humanity was inclusive. Despite being a Jewish male (he had to be something), Jesus was a figure who shares in the representational experiences of humanity. As the fourth-century theologian Gregory of Nazianzus pointed out, that which was not assumed was not healed.

> In the character of the form of a servant, He condescends
> to . . . take upon Him a strange form, bearing all me and mine
> in Himself, that in Himself He may exhaust the bad, as fire does
> wax, or as the sun does the mists of the earth, and that I may
> partake of His nature.[2]

Irenaeus was an early Christian writer who became Bishop of Lyons about the year 178 and died about the year 200. Writing in the Greek language, he was perhaps the first general theologian of the young church. His book *Against All Heresies* was a detailed attack on gnostic teaching that was threatening to derail Christianity. False teachers were questioning just how real was the humanity of Jesus. Irenaeus developed an intriguing defence of Jesus' full manhood. Irenaeus saw God's plan of salvation as a recapitulation of what was lost at the fall. The very Word of the Father came in fulfilment of 'God's comprehensive design' to be 'united and mingled with his handiwork' – us!

Look how Irenaeus develops the thought of Jesus identifying himself with us:

> He did not reject humanity or go beyond its limitations; he did not abrogate his laws for humanity in his own case; rather he sanctified each stage of life by a likeness to himself. He came to save all through his own person; all that is who through him are re-born to God; infants, children, boys, young men and old.
>
> Therefore, he passed through every stage of life. He was made an infant for infants, sanctifying infancy; a child among children, and setting an example of filial affection, of righteousness and of obedience, a young man among young men, becoming an example to them and sanctifying them in the Lord. So also, he was a grown man among the older men that he might be a perfect teacher for all.[3]

We could go further. Jesus sanctified every stage of life and the human condition in as broad a sweep as a single life could. He redeemed homeless people, he invested the routines of life with the qualities of God, redeeming education and singleness, and experiencing the sharp pangs of bereavement in order that he should be qualified as the Saviour of the grieving. 'Our Lord Jesus Christ, the Word of God, became what we are that he might make us what he himself is.'[4]

There has been a tendency in church history to see Jesus as a superman figure, or at least a Renaissance prince – a well-rounded man who has everything. Jesus did not have to be good at sport, good at his lessons, able to answer every question and get it right. If Jesus sailed across Galilee, we do not need to see him as the perfect sailor, any more than riding a donkey into Jerusalem means that Jesus was an expert horseman. His was a normal humanity, living out his secret identity until the time came to open the curtain and disclose it to the world. Until his baptism, Jesus lived quietly, and this is the real messianic secret.

Apocryphal stories want to turn Jesus into a purveyor of miracles when he was still a youngster. But the only moment when the hidden years gave anything away was the incident Luke records of Jesus visiting Jerusalem with his parents, just after adulthood, which meant he had become a partner in his Father's business. Then Luke simply records that 'he went down to Nazareth with them and was obedient to them' (Luke 2:51). And with that, the book is closed for another eighteen years.

Before he embarked on ministry, Jesus had already proved himself as a man (the Christian church would be better served if people first proved themselves as people). That's ten years of the routines of life in the real world for every year of active ministry. It's a proportion that underlines the genuineness of his humanity and the importance attached to it.

6

Anointed solidarity

As he embarked on his ministry, the human experiences of Jesus gathered in intensity. It was the empathy of God the Creator entering freely into what it means to be human; the sunlight and the gloom, the colour and the grey.

Then comes the anointing. The representative man will bring together water and Spirit, the washing of rebirth and renewal by the Holy Spirit (Titus 3:5). Israel had stood at key moments at a place where water and Spirit were brought together in powerful combination. At the very beginning of things, if ears could hear, the Spirit could be heard resting and brooding over creation's birth. The Exodus was enacted through cloud and sea (1 Corinthians 10:2). Prophetic anointing clothed Elisha on the banks of the Jordan when the mantle from the mentor fell on him (2 Kings 2:13).

The baptism of Jesus was the powerful curtain-raiser on his ministry as he stands in continuity with John's message and the story of Israel he will act out. The dove lights upon him; a voice was heard that combined two Old Testament scriptures

(both Psalm 2:7 and Isaiah 42:1) in a unique declaration of
Sonship that was to change the world. 'A voice came from
heaven: 'You are my Son, whom I love; with you I am well
pleased' (Luke 3:22). It marked him out. 'Beyond all question,
the mystery of godliness is great. He appeared in a body, was
vindicated by the Spirit' (1 Timothy 3:16).

Why Jesus chose to undergo baptism has always been a
mystery. After all, the rest of the Gospels show a flawless
character and an absence of sin that was unique in the annals
of the human race. Not even his enemies could accuse him of
sin. For the rest of us, when we are drawing near to God, we
are increasingly aware that the light exposes us. Not so with
Jesus. You will search the Gospels in vain for the slightest
confession of personal sin on his lips, any sense of throwing
himself upon God's righteous mercy.

Jesus certainly identified with John's movement, this remarkable mood that swept Judea around AD 26–27 when a rugged
preacher began to baptize true believers, not just Gentile
converts. A radical response to God was being called for; the
axe laid to the root of the trees. People had to get right with
God and show they were serious about repentance. It was all
to prepare the way for the Lord, the appearance of the Messiah;
the Messiah must therefore be a part of what was going on and
be initiated by it. Jesus could have been anointed for ministry
privately. But to be launched on the platform John provided
showed continuity with all that John was doing and would
build on its foundation.

But there is a deeper sense in which the baptism of Jesus
was an act of identification. Jesus is standing in solidarity
with the repentant. In obedience to God, Jesus is personally
undergoing what he will ask everyone else to do. He will
join them and set a pattern and example he personally
endorses.

Jesus was powerfully anointed as that dove came down upon him. The experience appeared gentle (dove rather than lightning bolt). But the anointing was so strong that it became the reference point for many years to come as the moment when amazing public ministry began.

'The Spirit encounter' was therefore an empowering encounter, not as God to God but the servant of Yahweh, the God-man. Solidarity with humanity is not enough. Standing shoulder to shoulder with what it is like to be human (or to be a refugee, one of a minority group, or to live on a council estate) is insufficient. Prophetic flame and the mysterious God-quality anointing must be present for the church, for churches that would follow on, and for the servants of the Lord in every generation.

Immediately, the representative man departs, but not to begin anointed ministry and announce the arrival of God's kingdom. Jesus leaves for the wilderness to do battle with the dark powers.

It was commonly agreed in the early church that Jesus was as subject to temptation as the next person, for he was the next person. But there was a time when temptation came in such concentration that anyone else would have been floored by its fierceness. Along with hunger, temptation came in rude knocks at the door of his mind that left him no peace. It was the old tempter; the old temptation.

Stones into bread! It was the temptation towards satisfying inner hunger in the wrong way. We are faced with this constantly, though for Jesus it would have been a magic trick in addition to meeting the gnawing hunger. God was not allowing him to eat at this time and certainly not this way.

'Look at all I can give you': the wealth of nations, the human ambition and the lust for power. It was all his for the taking, but Jesus refused, though he did not dispute that the world belonged temporarily to Satan. The devil's greatest coup would have been to have turned Jesus into the Antichrist. 'You don't want to go down this road. They're nothing but trouble. You're not going to do this for them. But if you persist in this ridiculous charade of being a human being, make it easy on yourself. There's a lot to be had down here. I can give you a share in it if you like.' Material possessions, position – it could be his, just like money, sex and power are there for the grabbing.

But there was no deal to be made, no bargain to be struck, and a desperate devil hit on a subtle trap that would appeal to the close relationship with the Father that Jesus prized far, far more than things. It's quite startling that at this very moment, the devil had Jesus under his power! 'The devil led him to Jerusalem and had him stand on the highest point of the temple' (Luke 4:9). Such was the reality of the onslaught and the storm that was raging around. But Jesus did not jump, even to prove that his Father would take care of him. The result would have been independence, not dependence.

'Everything in the world – the cravings of sinful man, the lust of his eyes and the boasting of what he has and does – comes not from the Father but from the world' (1 John 2:16). Jesus wasn't going to give in for anything or anyone. He must have felt the tug of his humanity and understood why all people, and good people, have gone down under it all. It was a repetition of the time when the first human beings were tempted. Like Jesus at a similar moment, Adam and Eve were faced with physical cravings (the fruit of the tree was good for food), their desire (it was pleasing to the eye) and the temptation to live independently from God (it was desirable for gaining wisdom).

Desire runs much of the known world. Jesus had to defeat the devil on the battleground of his humanity. The only weapons he was allowed were the weapons we have to fight with – everyday weapons of faith and prayer, God-dependence and the well-aimed use of Scripture. The really good news is that he did not need to resort to the weapons of his divinity or fall back on omnipotence. He defeated Satan with the kind of missiles and armour that humanity can also take up. In so doing, Jesus became tried and tested, steel forged in the heat, battle hardened. At the beginning of his ministry, Jesus had to know he could overcome his principal adversary and thereby overturn all the minor demons and scatter them from their perches like so many birds of the air. At the outset, Jesus won a major victory. Word quickly spread: 'I know who you are – the Holy One of God!' (Mark 1:24).

'When the devil had finished all this tempting, he left him until an opportune time' (Luke 4:13). Defeated by a mere man, the evil one strode off the stage of their single combat. He would be back when the man would be at his weakest. If Jesus was choosing to take the low road of pain rather than the high road of fame and fortune, Satan would sniff around for a suitable moment when pain was piling up.

This is why Jesus came across to his contemporaries as a good man, though more than a man, with radical integrity, obedience, courage, freedom and sheer victory. The goodness Jesus had was hard won out of the struggle with evil.

Walking the hard road

The pathway of identification continued. Jesus is God's selfie. When you look at Jesus you see God. But what Jesus had to contend with in his ministry is enough to strengthen the faint-hearted. Jesus knew what it was to feel the knife of **rejection**. 'All the people in the synagogue were furious when they heard this. They got up, drove him out of the town, and took him to the brow of the hill on which the town was built in order to throw him down the cliff' (Luke 4:28–29).

A **crowd** gets out of control. Jesus has experienced that fearful moment known to countless people down the centuries when a crowd assumed a life of its own and could turn nasty.

He attracted **opposition**: 'When Jesus left there, the Pharisees and the teachers of the law began to oppose him fiercely and to besiege him with questions, waiting to catch him in something he might say' (Luke 11:53–54). With all those who say 'They're always trying to catch me out or trip me up', Jesus identified.

Jesus knew what it was to be **spied on**, a watch kept on your every move, reported to the authorities. Jesus experienced that too: 'Keeping a close watch on him, they sent spies who pretended to be honest. They hoped to catch Jesus in something he said so that they might hand him over to the power and authority of the governor' (Luke 20:20).

Jesus was **vilified**: 'Every day, he was teaching at the temple. But the chief priests, the teachers of the law and the leaders among the people were trying to kill him' (Luke 19:47). He broke the rules and threatened to pull down the carefully structured spiritual culture built up to represent God: 'Indignant because Jesus had healed on the Sabbath, the synagogue ruler said to the people, "There are six days for work. So come and be healed on those days, not on the Sabbath"' (Luke 13:14).

Jesus was the subject of an **investigation**. A man born blind could see. Rather than be stunned into silence or begin to rejoice, his opponents felt it necessary to interrogate the miracle, explain it away, subject it to scrutiny and grill the grateful man. Listen to them investigating it: 'A second time they summoned the man who had been blind . . . Then they asked him, "What did he do to you? How did he open your eyes?" . . . Then they hurled insults at him' (John 9:24–28).

Jesus was berated as a **troublemaker**. Caiaphas was very eloquent on that subject, pouring scorn on those who wanted to tread carefully: 'You know nothing at all! You do not realise that it is better for you that one man die for the people than that the whole nation perish' (John 11:49–50).

Jesus was accused of **blasphemy**. That must have been especially gruelling for him, to be portrayed as slandering the Father he loved: 'At this, some of the teachers of the law said to themselves, "This fellow is blaspheming"' (Matthew 9:3). It was a charge that was to follow him around.

Commonly, routinely, he was **misunderstood**: 'When the Pharisees saw this, they said to him, "Look! Your disciples are doing what is unlawful on the Sabbath"' (Matthew 12:2). Why does it hurt to be misunderstood? Often we too have stood watching our own soul throb with this pain. What hurts is the contrast between how we want to stand for something, or come across, and how people perceive us. For misunderstanding to grieve us, one or other of two ingredients must be there. Either it must arise in a close relationship that then goes wrong and people start to read signals that were never intended, or it hurts if we have invested in a cause or stand for something that is important to us. When we invest something of ourselves we open up to the possibility of being misunderstood.

But there is more, much more. Jesus was **ostracized**. People had to come by night to talk to him. He was someone it wasn't good to be seen with. 'There was a man of the Pharisees named Nicodemus, a member of the Jewish ruling council. He came to Jesus at night and said, "Rabbi, we know you are a teacher who has come from God"' (John 3:1–2). 'Many even among the leaders believed in him. But because of the Pharisees, they would not confess their faith for fear they would be put out of the synagogue' (John 12:42). John adds a comment that sums it all up: 'They loved praise from men more than praise from God.'

Jesus experienced the pressure of **expectation**. This is a burden that has broken many backs, subtly controlling, shaping someone with an agenda that is foreign to them, disguised as praise but ultimately damaging, tying people up so they can't be themselves. How many have not survived the investiture of high hopes, wishes that no-one can fulfil, wishes that it would not be right to fulfil?

For Jesus knew the ups and downs of **popular opinion**, that to court it is to tread a risky road. Later in his ministry, John writes that 'From this time many of his disciples turned back and no longer followed him' (John 6:66). Five thousand people had just been fed from a boy's lunch box!

Then there were the **family pressures**: 'Now Jesus' mother and brothers came to see him, but they were not able to get near him because of the crowd. Someone told him, "Your mother and brothers are standing outside, wanting to see you"' (Luke 8:19–20). 'When his family heard about this, they went to take charge of him, for they said, "He is out of his mind"' (Mark 3:21).

Jesus identified with those who had failed and knew it. Jesus associated with those whom other people wrote off. Not only did he refuse to go first class, he went to the second-class carriage. 'I have not come to call the righteous, but sinners to repentance' (Luke 5:32), he said. Those who thought they were righteous already had no need of his message. Jesus went after those who knew they were blind rather than those who thought they could see. He gladly went to have a meal with a tax-collector. In those days, privatization had reached Inland Revenue. Tax-collectors were widely seen as milking their own people, betraying them with their greed that added on a little on the side, a bit here and there. 'All the people saw this and began to mutter, "He has gone to be the guest of a 'sinner'"' (Luke 19:7).

Jesus was having a meal with a Pharisee leader named Simon. What a commotion, what a gasp as the door flew open and the town prostitute threw herself down at the feet of Jesus to sob out the story of her broken and messy life. 'When the Pharisee who had invited him saw this, he said to himself, "If this man were a prophet, he would know who is touching him and what kind of woman she is – that she is a sinner"' (Luke 7:39).

A sordid past can be cleansed. Someone from the red-light district can be transformed by the white, bright light of God's power and love. Any and every human life can be redeemed. And those honest with God and with themselves will discover it and begin to love with vulnerability and passion. 'Her many sins have been forgiven – for she loved much. But he who has been forgiven little loves little' (Luke 7:47). Lacking a concept of redemption, those around Jesus did not understand that the gospel is a message for the moral failures.

Jesus had to endure **disappointment**. What a contrast between the high points – the feeding of a crowd, the raising of Lazarus, and so many other unforgettable moments – and the final days when it seemed like his movement lay in tatters around his whipped feet, and his mission had ended in ignominy, disgrace and tears. What a contrast between times when a lesser man would have basked in the adulation of the crowds and when Jesus is on trial for his life, and the Son of God is alone on the earth. Tell me that the story will end happily ever after and that the cross was not the end. We know that and he knew that, but say that the human side of Jesus did not cry out under the weight of broken dreams and disappointment and you say that his humanity was not real after all.

Jesus had to endure **the disciples**. They were slow to understand. Just when it looked like they were getting the message, they did something, said something, that was the opposite (Matthew 16:23). They were unspiritual men who needed to be softened and refined until they thought and reacted more like Jesus. How hard it was to go against the grain of their past and the influences that had shaped them. Caution! The disciples come in for a lot of stick in sermons. A very honest account of their struggle to grasp the significance of Jesus has been left on public record, not that they might be the butt of sermons but that we might see ourselves in them and identify with slow people.

And so often he was just **dog tired**. Jesus turned his back on creature comforts: 'Foxes have holes and birds of the air have nests, but the Son of Man has nowhere to lay his head' (Matthew 8:20). There was the constant pressure from crowds, people who wanted something from him, and pressure from his opponents who drained him, and it had been overwhelming at times. He was always on the go, tramping the highways and byways in pursuit of a rescue mission for the peoples of the earth.

Famished and weary, Jesus pauses beside a well hoping for some peace and respite. But it wasn't to be. 'Jesus, tired as he was from the journey, sat down by the well. It was about the sixth hour' (John 4:6). Along comes a Samaritan woman in the heat of the noonday sun and a dried-up life. Respite care is banished. From such events, Jesus carved ministry opportunities that shook entire villages. And it was love that wrought that carving. Love went on and on, without hindrance and without end.

This, then, is a broad sweep through some of the human experiences of Jesus. They don't need to tally with our experiences to be powerful to us when we go through similar things. What we are left with is resonance. Identification led him along a pathway marked by difficulty and discomfort.

But the pathway of identification was only at a half-way point.

*'In my judgement the adoption of the Chinese costume
would be desirable even if we were residing in the treaty ports,
but for work in the interior such as we contemplate, I am
satisfied that it is an absolute pre-requisite. No foreign
missionary has to the best of my knowledge ever carried on such
a work; and my strong conviction is that at present, no foreign
missionary could do so. He may travel under the protection of
his passport almost anywhere; but quietly to settle among the
people, obtaining free and familiar communication with them,
conciliating their prejudices, winning their esteem and
confidence, and so living as to be an example to them of what
Chinese Christians should be, requires adoption not merely of
their costume but of their habits to a very considerable extent.'*
Hudson Taylor, China Inland Mission[1]

7

The empathy of God

The journey continues

Decades later, Peter remembers the incident as if it were yesterday. The years have passed. So much has happened, but memory is vivid. Peter insists he is not spinning stories or embellishing incidents.

> We did not follow cleverly invented stories when we told you
> about the power and coming of our Lord Jesus Christ, but we
> were eyewitnesses of his majesty. For he received honour and
> glory from God the Father when the voice came to him from the
> Majestic Glory, saying, 'This is my Son, whom I love; with him
> I am well pleased.' We ourselves heard this voice that came from
> heaven when we were with him on the sacred mountain.
> (2 Peter 1:16–18)

That was the mountaintop. Down below waits a valley of need and the world of humanity for whom the Messiah must suffer and die. His transfiguration would have been a good place to finish the story except that the world could not have lived happily ever after. From such a peak experience, it was but a short step to heaven. But the Messiah turned his back on the glory that dazzled, to head straight for the mucky, grimy, sin-stained world below. The valley called. The road lay down rather than up. Jesus turned to embrace the way of the cross and the suffering and the glory – in that order.

Once, for a brief period of thirty-three years (a small chunk of the course of the world), God joined the human race. Jesus became one with us, one of us. But the empathy of God was not an end in itself, as if God showed himself here for a while and returned, having sampled human experience. Jesus was not the iconic heir to the estate, or like the nineteenth-century heir to Russian nobility who wanted to know what it would be like living as a son of the soil with the serfs. There must be a purpose in God being manifested in a human life far beyond bequeathing first-hand experience of being human.

The Gospels speak with a voice that is overwhelming in its loud consistency. The cross was central to why Jesus came. Jesus knew early on that his claims would be rejected and that the bridegroom would be taken away (Mark 2:20; 3:6). It could not be that a prophet could perish outside Jerusalem. The doctrine of a suffering Messiah was expressly laid out at Caesarea Philippi when Jesus forced the issue: 'Who do you say that I am?' Matthew sees this as a turning point: 'From that time on Jesus began to explain to his disciples that he must go to Jerusalem and suffer many things . . . that he must be killed and on the third day be raised to life' (Matthew 16:21).

What does the 'must' mean? Was it the inevitable outcome of the fatal situation that Jesus was in?

Mark then records Jesus saying that 'the Son of Man did not come to be served, but to serve, and to give his life as a ransom for many'. At the Last Supper, Jesus, knowing that death was inevitable but also indispensable, passed round a cup to express it: 'This is my blood of the covenant, which is poured out for many' (Mark 14:24). It was to be the climax to his ministry. He gave us a meal as a memorial.

Luke sees Jesus as a traveller on a journey – destination Jerusalem. 'As the time approached for him to be taken up to heaven, Jesus resolutely set out for Jerusalem' (Luke 9:51). It will be the culmination point of God's plan of salvation, which Luke is keen to stress in his opening chapters.

And John portrays Jesus as moving inexorably towards what he called 'my hour' (John 2:4, in the literal Greek). 'Now my heart is troubled, and what shall I say? "Father, save me from this hour"? No, it was for this very reason I came to this hour' . . . Jesus knew that the time had come for him to leave this world and go to the Father . . . "Father, the time has come"' (John 12:27; 13:1; 17:1).

The brotherhood of Christ

Hebrews 2 presents an exciting truth which we don't hear much about. In fact, I can't remember hearing a single sermon about it:

> For the one who sanctifies and those who are sanctified all have one Father. For this reason Jesus is not ashamed to call them brothers and sisters, saying,
> 'I will proclaim your name to my brothers and sisters,
> in the midst of the congregation I will praise you.'
> (Hebrews 2:11–12, NRSV)

Brothers! The fatherhood of God and the 'brotherhood of man' used to be great themes in the popular theology of the nineteenth century. But Jesus being our brother is at the heart of his identification with us. Jesus stands in essential solidarity with the human condition. He expresses God on earth, calling us brother and sister. Jesus is our point of contact with God. Baffled amazement deepens. He is not ashamed to call us brothers and sisters. Far too often, people have a problematic experience of fatherhood and then transpose those images on to God. But it is also true that Jesus stands as a brother with us. We share the same Father: 'For the one who sanctifies and those who are sanctified all have one Father' (Hebrews 2:11). We have a brother because we are adopted into the family.

There is another reason why Jesus stands in a relationship of brother – his identification with our humanity. We share a common humanity. We have a brother that we didn't know we had. Maybe if we could demonstrate more of the brotherhood of Jesus with humanity, the world would learn more about the fatherhood of God. 'Tell me what it's like for you', we can say to the broken lives living in a broken world at the dawn of the millennium. It will help us to make a connection with the outside.

We can be so set on a big-bang revival that will sweep everyone and everything into the Christian church that we miss the needs of those we see every day at work, or become uninterested in the messy human situations around us. God calls us to extend the incarnation by getting to know the people who play out their lives only a few feet away.

Jesus wore our clothes and looked like us. When God himself visited planet earth all those years ago, for thirty years hardly anyone noticed. Jesus was determined to learn the language and enter fully into our condition. From it he emerged with a deep understanding of people and a grasp of how the world worked on a level other than the spiritual (two requirements). He lived normally and naturally. God fitted into that culture. Maybe he can fit into any culture, even post-millennial Western culture.

Six hundred years before, Ezekiel had highlighted the importance of identifying with the people. Called to proclaim a strong message of collision between God and his own people, Ezekiel did not go straight to its delivery. 'I came to the exiles who lived at Tel Abib near the Kebar River. And there, where they were living, I sat among them for seven days – overwhelmed' (Ezekiel 3:15). He sat where they sat, feeling the tragedy of the collision, overwhelmed. Ezekiel is to be a watchman, a sentry on the tower with warning in his sad spirit and on his lips. Clouds on the horizon can only mean cataclysm; the drama of God's judgment. Identification with the people has become so close that his fortune is interwoven with theirs.

Or think of the spirit of the apostle Paul. Because he had tuned into the identification of Christ with a fallen world, he was prepared to change his identity. He became a chameleon Christian, adapting the presentation (though never the content) of the message to where his audience came from.

> Though I am free and belong to no man, I make myself a slave
> to everyone, to win as many as possible. To the Jews I became like
> a Jew, to win the Jews. To those under the law I became like one
> under the law (though I myself am not under the law), so as to
> win those under the law. To those not having the law I became
> like one not having the law (though I am not free from God's law
> but am under Christ's law), so as to win those not having the law.
> (1 Corinthians 9:19–21)

Or think of the Christian missionary Hudson Taylor who opened up inland China for the good news. Hudson Taylor warned that adoption of the Chinese costume was not just an external identification.

> Merely to put on their dress and act regardless of their thoughts and feelings is to make a burlesque of the whole matter, and will probably lead the person so adopting it to conclude, before long, that it is of very little value to him. But I have never heard of any one, after a bona fide attempt to become Chinese to the Chinese that he might gain the Chinese, who either regretted the course taken or wished to abandon it.[2]

Identification is not skin deep. Adoption of persona is central to the move. It occasioned much comment at that time. Was it really necessary to 'go native'? In a letter back home to help candidates for the Mission think it through, Hudson Taylor explained why the step was in the spirit of Jesus:

> Had our Lord appeared on earth as an angel of light, he would doubtless have inspired far more awe and reverence, and would have gathered even larger multitudes to attend His ministry. But to save man, he became man, not merely like man . . . In language, in appearance, in everything not sinful He made Himself one with those He sought to benefit.

Hudson Taylor was a trendsetter. Making good news look foreign in dress and everything else

> has hindered rapid dissemination of the Truth among the Chinese. And why should such a foreign aspect be given to Christianity? The Word of God does not require it; not could sound reason justify it. It is not the de-nationalisation of this people but the Christianisation of this people that we seek. We wish to see Chinese Christians raised up – men and women truly Christian but truly Chinese.[3]

A debate that will never be settled until the end comes is how far the church should move with the times. To some people, for whom the highest value is truth, that sounds immediately like compromise. For others, truth is definitely top of the list but having an outward-looking vision to reach lost people is also of prime importance. How you hear this and rank these values reflects your background and determines your practice. Sadly, tragically, the Christian scene is full of monuments and statues. We have not been taught to think in terms of moving with the times. We must hold on to the truth, for there aren't many of us about who do. We wouldn't think like that if we studied the identification of Jesus more closely. If we did, it would re-educate us to want to make more of a connection with those around us. In a constantly changing culture, truth cannot walk unclothed.

A discovery awaits us if we grapple with this seriously. It will sink in that those who prided themselves on just being biblical were usually oblivious to how much their own form of culture had affected them. New Testament Christianity has expressed itself in countless different ways throughout history, each type believing it was authentic. And why not, for each person is an individual and each expression of Christianity begins by fitting into a particular society.

On the day we learn that even the form of Christianity we like best is but a culture-bound approximation to the good news, something will happen. Realizing that all along we were speaking *from* our own culture will equip us to speak to it. That is where we live. We speak its language but we also try with faltering lips to speak the language of heaven. We will be released, first, to think critically about our own expression of church while being grateful for it (it has met a real need and it suits many). Then we will be free to engage with the world around. Mission is messy. It means thinking through our boundaries. To reach the weak may mean we wear the clothes of fading strength, but to reach lap dancers does not mean we apply for their job.

In being a son of Israel, Jesus retold the story of Israel as his own. In later theological terms, the transcendent God became immanent in a particular person and at a particular time and place. But the theology only expresses a deep truth. God has emerged from the objectivity and come to our side. He has stepped out from behind the mists of what is unseen in order to be seen and felt and handled. In stepping out, Jesus became a man of the people.

If only Christians could be known for this. Why can't we have such love for people that we are genuinely interested to understand as much as we can about what makes someone else tick and what motivates them? Jesus walked this way. Wherever we have a need we have a choice. Circumstances may limit the opportunity or the appropriateness of our ministry. But though we may not respond impulsively, the call on our hearts must be compulsive. Jesus was involved.

The humble sublime

In serving rather than being served, the Son of Man left the most powerful example that could be given: 'Now that I, your Lord and Teacher, have washed your feet, you also should wash one another's feet' (John 13:14). This was the Jesus style. And it explodes self-sufficiency and becomes a pattern of ministry precisely because it was the story of Jesus' life and that amazing stoop.

> Do nothing out of selfish ambition or vain conceit, but in humility consider others better than yourselves . . . Your attitude should be the same as that of Christ Jesus: Who being in very

nature God, did not consider equality with God something
to be grasped, but made himself nothing, taking the very nature
of a servant. (Philippians 2:3, 5–7)

But there was more. The stoop was to continue: 'And being
found in appearance as a man, he humbled himself and
became obedient to death – even death on a cross' (2:8).

His humility becomes a pattern of service: 'I have set
you an example that you should do as I have done for you'
(John 13:15).

8

The day of crushing

In the pathway of identification, there was some very rough territory to go through. 'Going a little farther, he fell with his face to the ground and prayed, "My Father, if it is possible, may this cup be taken from me. Yet not as I will, but as you will"' (Matthew 26:39).

From the Arabic *gat semen*, Gethsemane was 'an olive press'. It was where Jesus accepted the cup offered to him and where he was to be crushed alive. 'He took Peter and the two sons of Zebedee along with him, and he began to be sorrowful and troubled. Then he said to them, 'My soul is overwhelmed with sorrow to the point of death. Stay here and keep watch with me"' (Matthew 26:37–38).

The place of the press was where the agony of human redemption pressed upon him so strongly that he was being crushed for oil to flow for the world. Already sorrowful, Jesus began to be overwhelmed. Matthew says Jesus was troubled (*adēmonein*, deeply depressed). And, in the depths of heaviness of spirit, Jesus was a community of one alone, as happens when we suffer. All troubles seem very lonely places. No-one else can quite feel and know what we are going through.

Jesus knew at that moment the experiences of 300 million in our world at the beginning of the third millennium who suffer from malignant sadness, condemned to dragging dark and heavy days around with them. Jesus knew what it was to be immersed in sorrow so deep that he went under and was almost drowned. He not only tasted sadness and depression of spirit, Jesus ate it to the full and drank the cup dry. He knew what it is like when the battery runs out.

In the garden at the beginning of things, the Son had been there with the Father and the Spirit as the first humans were tempted and failed. Now, three men look on as Jesus wrestles against overwhelming pressure and temptation to escape what was to befall him. In the garden, Jesus prevailed over temptation where the first man went down under it. But Jesus fought and won as a man, not just as God. It was far, far more than fear of pain. The sorrows of Jesus were in a different dimension, infinitely more profound and vast, wider and deeper. Jesus was to take on his shoulders the sins of the world. No wonder it was breaking his humanity, the olive crushed in the press.

Jesus became the representative human being, embracing all in order to redeem, persevering in those final hours of identification. He knew the knife of betrayal:

> While they were eating, he said, 'I tell you the truth, one of you will betray me.' They were very sad and began to say to him one after the other, 'Surely not I, Lord?' . . . 'The one who has dipped his hand into the bowl with me will betray me . . . Woe to that man who betrays the Son of Man . . . Look, the hour is near and the Son of Man is betrayed into the hands of sinners. Rise, let us go! Here comes my betrayer!' (Matthew 26:21–24, 45–46)

When John wrote about this, he was reminded of an old psalm that captures the agony of betrayal in a single verse. Three thousand years have passed and you can still see the blood pouring from soul-wounds: 'Even my close friend, whom I trusted, he who shared my bread, has lifted up his heel against me' (Psalm 41:9). How could he do it? It hurt so much more that it was someone close whom he had spent time with and opened his heart and table to. If it was an enemy he could understand it. But it was his friend!

How could they do this to me? It is the cry of the executive when the knives in the back come from someone you thought you had an alliance with, the cry of a spouse whose partner has had an affair, the cry of parents when their own children turn against them, the cry of those who are left when someone takes their life in an act of selfish desperation. It was the cry of Jesus when Judas walked out into the night.

Judas betrayed Jesus, and Peter disowned him. Why is such a contrast drawn between these two men? Both let Jesus down enormously and failed. Denial – 'I don't know the man' – sounds a bit like betrayal. But the Gospels insist on the different moral quality of their actions. Peter didn't stand with Jesus – Judas stood against him. Peter couldn't rise to the occasion in a moment of panic and cowardice. Judas actively plotted against Jesus. But Judas was broken by remorse and saw no way back, whereas heartbroken Peter was personally reinstated by the very one he had denied.

When everyone else walks out the back door, Jesus walks in the front door. He knew what it was to be disowned and enters into the experience.

The sequence of events is well known to us. The experience of identification is replete with milestones that have been spoken about for centuries.

Jesus was put on trial. It was of course a trumped-up trial with trumped-up charges. They falsely accused him and twisted his words. He had never said, 'I am able to destroy the temple of God and rebuild it in three days' (Matthew 26:61). Those words kept being thrown back in his face (27:40). It was a miscarriage of justice and Pilate acknowledged it to be so: 'I find no basis for a charge against this man' (Luke 23:4). Jesus was kicked to and fro like a football between the Sanhedrin, Herod and Pilate before the inevitable ensued.

There came the moment when Jesus stood before the crowd at the judgment seat of Pilate, wearing the crown of thorns and the purple robes. 'Here is the man,' declared Pilate. '*Ecce homo* – Behold the man!' (John 19:5). It is but a glimpse, but it conjures up unforgettable imagery of the first man strutting around in independence of God in the very place where the thorns come up. Jesus stands in the place of proud humanity, wearing a crown and the imperial purple, enduring the ignominy and the shame. The old Adam humanity is being adopted in full measure but will soon be relegated.

Jesus experienced being mocked and insulted: 'The soldiers twisted together a crown of thorns and put it on his head. They clothed him in a purple robe and went up to him again and again, saying "Hail, king of the Jews!" And they struck him in the face' (John 19:2–3); 'Falling on their knees, they paid homage to him' (Mark 15:19).

With every step, the going on the pathway of identification got harder. Jesus knew what it was to have a crowd yelling for your last drop of blood (Luke 23:18), the nation that he had wept over and sought to rescue from being trapped by their traditions, from sin and from disaster. The world rejected the Son of God and the Prince of Peace, and called for a murderer in his place. It got what it wanted. In the end, Pilate 'surrendered Jesus to their will' (Luke 23:25).

For all those who have faced crowds and lynch mobs, Jesus suffered.

Stumbling and throbbing, Jesus bore the cross as long as he could. Strength gave out. A visitor from Libya was recruited to carry the cross in his place (Mark 15:21; Romans 16:13). The event changed Simon for ever, for, spiritually, it was the other way round and Jesus bore it for him.

For all those who have reached the end of their tether, Jesus walked that road.

Everything was taken from him. They even bargained for his clothing. For all those who have been looted or lost everything, Jesus stands in solidarity. But the pathway of identification was still descending, going down and down.

The pain of his ordeal on the cross was intense. So why was the form of his execution one of the most excruciating ever devised? The nails through the wrists were only the beginning. His body sagged down under its own weight until the urge to snatch a breath forced him upwards – and the deathly cycle began again. It was six hours of torture. To be nailed on a pole and hung out naked before the sun – this was what they did to Jesus when he identified with humanity. But the physical anguish was only a surface wound. 'At the ninth hour Jesus cried out in a loud voice, "*Eloi, Eloi, lama sabachthani?*" – which means, "My God, my God, why have you forsaken me?"' (Mark 15:34).

Rejection, desolation, was the cup on offer to Jesus in those six hours. He drank it with stark, sharp images of broken people and their broken dreams staring back at him, dreams from rejected second-class people who crowd the centuries, who filled every time, every age, every generation, every country, every town and every street. He drank it for the child in the womb shaped not in an oasis of security but amid a thousand discordant noises that pierced the primeval ocean with unease, giving an indefinable sense of foreboding to the life ahead.

The pain forced a cry unique to him, new and strange, profoundly unsettling. As the sun went dark, a cloud swept over the soul of his humanity. He was alone. Even the Father was out of reach.

Was Jesus aware at that moment of the old humanity in whose shape and likeness he came? As he endured his ordeal, was Jesus mindful of the moment when Adam suddenly experienced a strange, unbrave new world of guilt, self-consciousness and separation? On that other day, with the other tree, he had become man-forsaken God. Now to put it right he was to be a God-forsaken man, nailed to a tree that would become the tree of life.

Jesus was experiencing first hand the vulnerable nakedness of the derelict sufferer who pours out his soul to God but feels that God is far away. Bearing the sin of a whole world upon him, Jesus knew that even the Father would turn his back at that moment. Jesus experienced the withdrawal of the face of God. It was the first time he had ever known the absence of God and it drew from deep inside the holy well of his being a cry that was profoundly unsettling. For three hours, the sun stopped shining and the Father ceased smiling. And it had all been envisaged in writing, years ago.

Travails of the innocent sufferer

Calvary was for Jesus an immersion into malice and cruelty. Stripped, Jesus was vulnerable to their violence. He trod the pathway of the vulnerable throughout history, the weak and those who have become a target for bullying and cruelty. Jesus knew who now, not from the outside looking in but from the inside looking out. Humiliation was mixed in the cup Jesus was drinking. 'I can count all my bones; people stare and gloat over me. They divide my garments among them and cast lots for my clothing' (Psalm 22:17–18). Stripped of all his possessions, Jesus was left with nothing. How humiliating for the Son of God to be treated in that way. This was no criminal to be degraded; this was God on earth, the holiest of all holy prophets, the most loving and best of all good men.

That's why Psalm 22 can bring the liberating power of the cross to people in such a profound way. Other psalms of dereliction also applied to Jesus that day and can help us.

What Jesus was enduring had to be borne alone. The pathway of identification lay through all those desperately dark and difficult dry places until all was accomplished.

Now his work was done, Jesus could yield to death. His suffering had touched all the states of human life and now he dies as human beings are obliged to do. As the writer to those Jewish Christians put it, he suffered death 'so that by the grace of God he might taste death for everyone' (Hebrews 2:9, NRSV).

One of the surprising features of much theological analysis of the death of Christ is that it draws heavily and rightly on Paul but neglects the way the Gospels present the destiny Jesus knew was imminent. The meaning Jesus brought to the death he knew was awaiting him in Jerusalem is profoundly instructive. Jesus hosted a meal for his followers pregnant with significance. He himself interpreted his own death. He had predicted it. Now he slips into it.

'The curtain of the Temple was torn in two. Jesus called out with a loud voice, "Father, into your hands I commit my spirit." When he had said this, he breathed his last' (Luke 23:46). He knew he was an innocent sufferer. Leaping into the abyss, he made a supreme act of trust, knowing that God would raise him up. 'My body also will live in hope, because you will not abandon me to the grave, nor will you let your

Holy One see decay' (Psalm 16:9–10, quoted by Peter in Acts 2:26–27). 'Later, knowing that all was now completed, and so that the Scripture would be fulfilled, Jesus said, "I am thirsty." . . . When he had received the drink, Jesus said, "It is finished." With that, he bowed his head and gave up his spirit' (John 19:28, 30).

But what was accomplished, and what was finished?

'[On the cross,] God made the sinless Messiah to "be sin" on our behalf. All our sins, our failings, our inadequacies, were somehow dealt with there, so that we – the apostles, and all who are called to be "ministers of reconciliation" – could embody in our own lives the faithfulness of God.'
Tom Wright[1]

9

Redemption through violence: interpreting the cross

As we consider the message of the cross, an inescapable reality dominates the skyline. At the heart of Christian faith lies an act of horrific violence.

To its detractors, Islam has an enduring problem with violence that stains the landscapes of the contemporary world. Other religions, including those that profess peace, have a violent streak. Yet the red mark of Cain has stained Christian history no less. Crimes committed in the name of the Prince of Peace fill the centuries. It is all the more startling to realize that the world was redeemed by violence.

Immersion into violence reflected the human situation. The new century is racked by pain; stained by blood and injustice. Syria's torment (where a callous regime saw only terrorism in the people's demands for justice) was bad enough. But no conflict since the end of the Second World War surpasses the Congo carnage. Rwandan genocide stoked it. Terrifying war at the heart of Africa, where war lords fuel tribal bloodbaths, where Kalashnikov children rule the streets and where rape is weaponized, took its toll in blood. No one has counted the corpses. The problems of humanity refuse to dissolve; the cry of a lonely planet grows stronger and louder as the years unfold and the heart of God continues to break. 'I have indeed seen the misery of my people in Egypt. I have heard them crying out because of their slave drivers, and I am concerned about their suffering. So I have come down to rescue them' (Exodus 3:7).

A God who is concerned about human suffering? That is hardly the image twenty-first-century people have of God. Persistently, consistently, the pain of the tortured human situation is paraded by those who can relate neither to God nor to his church. The problem of suffering they call it. A smokescreen it may be. But unless people can see God as someone they can relate to in their lives even in the dark places, they will stand aside from believing in him.

Because it is so perennial and so personal (for it touches us all), the problem of suffering has drawn the attention of the greatest minds in history. Theologians and armchair phil-osophers debate the subject endlessly. Why suffering is allowed into the system is the focus for God-rejection by the crowds. Amid the responses that can and should be made, there is one response that is distinctively Christian. Leave this out and the good news has not been brought to bear on the problem. The Creator has embraced the very suffering he has allowed into the system. No-one can accuse him of non-involvement. The symbol of Christian faith is the cross, not a celestial deckchair. This is God standing in solidarity with the kind of world we have made for ourselves.

It stands in contrast to other world faiths and their message to the world. Eastern religions have been fatalistic about suffering. Lepers and sick people, the lower castes and the generally less fortunate are all working out their karma from the last time round. Their previous existence brings a resigned attitude in the present. There is inevitability about it. Why should they be helped? Yet Jesus was indignant.

In the wake of Auschwitz, some have written about 'the pain of God' or 'the crucified God'. These are evocative phrases. If the awfulness of the Holocaust has not challenged us profoundly, we have not thought deeply enough. For the pain of God demonstrated at the cross connects radically and powerfully with the world's pain. The longer you look at the cross, the more you are moved and influenced by it. It's an incredibly powerful demonstration, an unforgettable statement that has etched its way into the fabric of our Western civilization: the identification principle in full measure. 'God demonstrates his own love for us in this: While we were still sinners, Christ died for us' (Romans 5:8). Yet there is more in the cross even than the most powerful statement that can be conceived.

It was taking a long hard look at the cross that moved Isaac Watts to write the ending of his immortal hymn: 'Love so amazing, so divine, demands my soul, my life, my all.'

Undeniably, the ordeal of the crucifixion has great power to move and stir us. The cross whispers to us that God's love is the greatest force in the universe, greater by far than animosity and violence. God's love can cross the bridge. Self-sacrificing divine love strikes a chord within us as we are moved by what God has done. Jesus made simple goodness, love and humility more powerful than nuclear weapons. A world stained red with violence must grasp that urgently. Yet there is more.

Jesus followed the twentieth century into the anguish of human extremity and pain. He was there with them in the gas chamber while they closed the doors. He went with us into bereavement and into cancer, with every victim of war and injustice, and with every mother caring for her disabled child with a heavy heart. No darkness can keep its doors barred against a self-sacrificing love that accomplishes the redemption of the world. Here is identification at its most intense. The pain of God connects with the children of the genocide generation and a world pursuing the madness of violence and rape of the environment. Enduring Christ-love pursues us into the twenty-first century with its tattered social order, with terrorism and territory in the land of his birth rent asunder in anguish. Despite the post-millennial West giving up on God, God is no stranger to the complex agony of humanity. Calvary tells us that our condition became his; redeeming outside the city, though insider to its lore and its core. Yet there is more.

We have tracked the full-time, complete immersion project into the wilderness regions of random cruelty. Jesus drank of the lived experience of every day. He ate to the full what life is like on ground level. The cross of Christ constitutes maximum exposure to the envy, greed, strife and lust that stalk the human heart. The closer we look at the empathy of God, the more we are moved by the degree of his identification. A cursory glance will not do anything for us. The more we concentrate on it, the more we become convinced that the kind of selfish, cruel strife that claimed Jesus as victim is not how we should live our lives. Jesus was the supreme exemplar of love in the face of suffering and of the power of goodness: a role model that gently prises open fingers of selfishness. We look at the self-sacrifice of Jesus and we say, 'Here is the solidarity of God with the victims' – and we are all victims. The gaunt faces of the tortured, the emaciated faces of the famished, the frightened, lonely faces of the refugees – these are his type of people. God is calling us to make a connection and become the face of God. Unfortunately, the situation is more complex. We are also perpetrators.

Until recent times, much of the Christian church had little to say about violence. It was a vicious example, among many, of flawed and fallen humanity. Yet it is more. Violence is fundamental to the need for atonement and redress because it is about the forcible devaluation of humankind, one to the other, whether in word or deed. A theology of violence is long overdue. It is easier to talk about sin in general, or individual moral failure, rather than get down grubby and bloody.

The victims of violence have experienced a jagged reality that is all around, pervasive in militancy. With searing abrasiveness, they have encountered power: the power that is at the heart of the darkness and the dark powers. In its lashing, they come up against the wanton essence of sin; the proud primordial power that stands over against God. Gratuitously scraping the value off the face of another as a china plate can be marked – this is what sin does in violent, mocking disregard.

Jesus was a real person going through real things. He was on the receiving end of the most brutal form of violence that can be imagined. This is no accident. The Gospels do not portray Jesus as gathering his followers around him and drinking hemlock as did Socrates. Death by crucifixion (after flogging that left him in a weakened condition) was searing, unrelenting and bloody. Did it have to be this way? Yes – for unless violence could be redeemed, the scope of the cross would be limited. The sting has completely gone because it has been absorbed. One side of the cross is wanton cruelty, all the more savage for its being sport as well as judicious public execution. At the cross springs forgiveness.

Would it have worked if Jesus had merely sipped poison and perished? Did it have to be so brutal? Violence converted into forgiveness – this is an important way of understanding the cross of Christ. Forgiveness rather than an eye for an eye is fully and authentically Christian. Jesus takes the violence directed at him – and in its place flows a powerful technology with which to disarm our world.

There are ways of seeing the cross of Christ. Some stress that Jesus does not so much take the blame for us as stand *with us* amid our sinfulness. The spirit of this emphasis is **participation**. It is not that Jesus is there in our place so much as standing in solidarity with the human situation, bearing the kind of things we have to do and transforming them. Jesus takes the worst that violence and grim toxicity can inflict on anyone, and turns it into love. He redeems not by being the saviour figure from outside but living where we live and taking the violent rubbishing because he identifies with our humanity. Jesus becomes one with the innocent person incarcerated in a concentration camp; he becomes one with those faced with hatred and greed and shows us a better way, a way out.

Staunch advocates of **substitution** (whereby Jesus suffers and dies in our place) stress that God is *for us*. Jesus takes the place of the sinning man and woman. He dies instead of them; bears the punishment on their behalf and in their place so they can go free. Jesus takes the worst but transforms it by being both representative participant and unique scapegoat. In fact, there is less contrast here than many have thought. Some versions of Christianity have tended to stress solidarity rather than substitution; that God is *with us* in suffering and the banality of evil to enable us to rise above them and turn us to the power of righteous love, the victory that vindicates. Those seeking above all to be faithful to Scripture have emphasized that God is *for us* as a sacrifice for sin.

Both perspectives turn on the idea of solidarity. They trace the incarnation of Jesus to the point where he is fully one with the human condition, including the confrontation with extreme violence. Jesus is not being human only at the cross where he is the scapegoat, accused and brutalized. He comes to his own all the way along the path. From cradle to grave, Jesus is one with humanity.

With all the approaches, the reason why the atonement works is through the identification principle. Jesus represents God becoming one with us, one of us, one for us. The atonement is a development of the incarnation. The former is derived from the latter. Jesus becoming one with the human situation at Christmas goes on inexorably to its nadir at the first Easter.

The weakness of God

> God's foolishness is wiser than human wisdom, and God's
> weakness is stronger than human strength. (1 Corinthians 1:25,
> NRSV)

The weakness of God! It is an astounding statement, quite unique to Christianity. Paul explains how the weak God shows up the apparent strength and superiority that whole cultures can flaunt.

The cross teaches a macho culture where its true strength lies; the cross teaches laddish cultures to admit the weakness that dare not emerge. Through the cross, the weakness of God becomes a point of contact with our times. Here is a Christ we can relate to, a Christ whose strength does not repel but whose weakness attracts (providing we recognize our own).

What seemed to be ultimate weakness and an act of shame on God's part had just been used to save the world. It had just happened. What seemed to be the death of a criminal had been converted into a message of salvation and hope. Powerful sophisticated people would rather not be saved by such a message. Maybe Paul should have downplayed the cross and coughed at that point. But he refused to. At the cross, a place of shame was a means of glory, and weakness was a channel of power.

Why have we missed the weakness of God, preferring the mighty king or spirit-empowered charismatic? Paul saw it, and the spirit of Paul will move the twenty-first-century world if we make the necessary connection. By any yardstick, Paul was God's man of faith and power. Yet the weakness of God influenced him profoundly to live out a paradox: 'I came to you in weakness and fear, and with much trembling. My message and my preaching were not with wise and persuasive words, but with a demonstration of the Spirit's power' (1 Corinthians 2:3–4). He writes about the paradox in his second letter to the Corinthian church, a church that needed to learn how much pride, worldly wisdom and superiority always come with factions. Watch the self-disclosure, the point of weakness, the paradox he hopes will woo them and attract them.

Excursion – By way of background

Ask church folk why the blood of Christ was necessary and they will tell you about the Old Testament and sacrifices that involved the shedding of blood to forgive people. But that is to argue in a circle. Why does it take sacrifice of any sort to deal with wrongdoing, whether in Old Testament times or New Testament times? Yet an understanding of the atonement cannot be separated from notions of guilt and forgiveness. This is why the Old Testament background is important.

In the twentieth century, it was fashionable for theologians and other Christians to ridicule this understanding of the death of Christ. The idea that a blood sacrifice was needed to save us seemed at odds with the sophisticated civilization we had become. To say that God would only forgive people because of the death of his Son was antiquated. Talk of the sacrifice of lambs and emphasizing the blood of Jesus is surely the theology of the butcher's shop. Saying that Jesus took the blame that should have been ours is to keep in circulation the currency of a morally inferior doctrine.

Modern detractors abound. It is well known that talk of sacrifice and penalty can hardly get a hearing today. Those crude accounts of Christian doctrine that say that Christ has been justly punished in our place so that he has taken away our guilt and enabled God to forgive us are surely to be rejected. Or are they? We are told that Christ did not die for our sins, that the church's traditional teaching on the crucifixion is repulsive and insane. The idea that Jesus was sent to earth to die in atonement for the sins of humankind makes God sound like a psychopath. Is it better to say that Jesus was crucified so he could share in the worst of grief and suffering that life can throw at us? In short, Jesus identifies with us. This still offers some notion of substitution, Jesus dying in our place. The difference is that in the idea of Jesus sharing the tragic horror of life, there is no thought of penalty.

Jesus 'dying in our place' could mean:

1. *Dying as one of us* – that is, experiencing the full horror of the human situation as anyone else has to, especially victims of violence and injustice.
2. *Dying with us* – Jesus taking on himself the death and violence that came up with the human condition but alongside us, not instead of us.
3. *Dying instead of us* – Jesus taking our place as the Just and Righteous One, thus enabling the unjust to be acquitted (1 Peter 3:18). Jesus bears human guilt and punishment, not just the human condition. This is substitution. There is a penalty that is due and Jesus pays it in full.

Substitution is someone doing something in the place of another, the third of these. A football player comes on at half-time as a substitute for someone else; they are not playing on the field at the same time. But he or she is a full participant in the team. The atonement is about substitution *and* participation. Jesus is inserted into the human situation as the sin-bearer *instead of us*. What took place there becomes load-bearing. We do not have to carry that load or its consequences.

'Cur Deus homo?' asked Anselm back in the Middle Ages. Why did God become human? And he comes to the conclusion that the cross achieves forgiveness. Each theologian writing on these matters paid attention to Scripture, but also reflected their experiences and the social setting of their age.

Making sense of the cross went far beyond the need to find some kind of meaning in sad events such as unexpected bereavement, or tragic events marked by unredeemed suffering. Biblical writers were compelled to wrap meaning around the death of Jesus because of who they perceived him to be. When it comes to Paul's theology of the cross, five themes stand out:

- worship: sacrifice (1 Corinthians 5:7; Romans 3:25)
- battleground: triumph over evil (Galatians 1:4; Colossians 2:15)
- the court room: justification (Romans 3:21 – 4:25; 1 Corinthians 1:30)
- the marketplace: redemption (Ephesians 1:7; Colossians 1:14)
- reconciliation and personal relationships (2 Corinthians 5:18–19; Colossians 1:20–21)

The way that Paul weaves these themes together shows there is underlying unity. Jesus did not die five times for five different reasons. Massive thinker as he was, Paul did not develop a systematic way to make sense of the death of Christ. That was the task of church theologians down the ages. Scripture does not play on one string when it comes to how we make sense of Calvary. Evangelical commentators focus on Paul's writings for understandable reasons, but there is a wealth of meaning in what Jesus said about his approaching death and the terms on which he interpreted it (parables in the second half of Matthew, or the Last Supper where Jesus gave us a meal to remember him and where Matthew 26:28 echoes Isaiah 53:12 – the Servant Song of the identification principle).

The suffering Servant

The suffering Servant is a figure for the twenty-first century.

The Servant of the Lord calmly bears what others have done to him. He is innocent, enduring personal catastrophe for others, not suffering because he was guilty. 'Surely he took up our infirmities and carried our sorrows, yet we considered him stricken by God, smitten by him, and afflicted' (Isaiah 53:4).

This part of the Servant Song is quoted by Matthew, to show that messianic promises were fulfilled in Jesus. '[Jesus] drove out the spirits with a word and healed all the sick. This was to fulfil what was spoken through the prophet Isaiah, "He took up our infirmities and carried our diseases"' (Matthew 8:16–17).

Here is depicted the sympathetic suffering of Jesus and the way he voluntarily embraced the pain and distress of humanity. Because Jesus identified himself so closely with us right where it hurts, he applies power to restore the broken places. The one who came alongside a wounded world can heal.

All the human experiences of Jesus were vicarious, endured on behalf of others, arising from the conditions he imposed on himself. His acceptance of the condition of humanity reached all the way to where those experiences were most intense. At the cross, Jesus knew what it was to experience rejection, mockery, anguished humiliation, desolation and, especially, separation from the Father. The death and sufferings of the One for others connects with our lives. The innocent sufferer of Isaiah 53 takes up our infirmities and carries our sorrows. Through what is done to him, he enters into what others have done to us. He is identifying with the innocent sufferers who crowd history.

The rejection that he experienced, the way he climbed into mockery and humiliation, the way he was pierced by the betrayal that knifes us, his immersion into cruelty and descent into darkness – all this showed an intense identification with the human condition. It was our betrayal, our rejection, our cruelty and our mockery that he was drinking deeply, humbled with our humiliation.

The good news not only addresses fundamental human concerns, it addresses fundamental human needs. But there is more. The innocent sufferer is not only identifying with the sufferers, he is identifying with those who cause suffering. He is standing in the place of the guilty.

> But he was pierced for our transgressions, he was crushed for our iniquities; the punishment that brought us peace was upon him, and by his wounds we are healed. We all, like sheep, have gone astray, each of us has turned to his own way; and the LORD has laid on him the iniquity of us all. (Isaiah 53:5–6)

In his death, Jesus became one with suffering humanity in its entirety, in the full spectrum of human experience. But he also identified with the effects, the suffering that is a consequence of our sin or someone else's, what others have done to us. Jesus

Christ became one with the cause of sorrow; the sin that has corrupted God's way on the earth, what we have done to others (the other strand of the rope that weaves the complexity of our problems).

The suffering Servant is not suffering for the innocent but for the guilty, not endorsing what they have done or agreeing with it but drawing it down on himself. 'He had done no violence', though condemned through violence along with men and women of violence.

What is the unseen explanation of the anguished Servant, with its sonorous but strangely hopeful tone? Yahweh has appointed his Servant to be a guilt-offering, but he can see beyond the crisis. The Servant is, as it were, in the throes of childbirth, but children will definitely come as a result (Isaiah 53:10). Many will be accepted because he was rejected (53:11). The anguish closes in on the Servant now and his life ebbs away. But there will be victory spoils 'because he poured out his life unto death, and was numbered with the transgressors' (53:12). This is identification.

This Servant Song came so readily to be applied to Jesus since the impetus came directly from him – the healings of Jesus in sympathetic power, the Last Supper, then this. 'Did not the Christ have to suffer these things and then enter his glory? And beginning with Moses and all the Prophets, he explained to them what was said in all the Scriptures concerning himself' (Luke 24:26–27).

The death of Jesus was not the unfortunate and premature ending of a spiritual leader. It was an act of identification, an act that connects so profoundly with the human situation it offers transforming power. 'He bore the sin of many, and made intercession for the transgressors' (Isaiah 53:12). This is referred to in the words of the institution of communion during the Last Supper (Matthew 26:28).

This is especially harrowing when a biblical picture of sin is taken on board. Sin is not about making a few mistakes. It is a disease in the human heart, affecting the mind, will and the emotions.

Two thousand years ago, a man was crucified. One man among three crucified that morning at that location; one crucifixion among hundreds no doubt sentenced to capital punishment that day in the Roman Empire; one crucifixion among several million in the ancient world. Pinning Jesus to a piece of wood one Friday morning was like any other death. Yet it was a crucifixion like any other and none other. Somehow, that single crucifixion, those personal sufferings and that one death have global significance and are able to save the world. That at least is the Christian claim.

The Bible portrays the death of Jesus as a death for others, an act of solidarity with the human race; Jesus died to save a world that had rejected God and turned its back on him. We are to go and make a connection between this supreme act of identification and the trapped generation that live at the dawn of the third millennium.

This is the full understanding of the atonement, that the cross was designed to affect human beings because first and foremost it influences God. Jesus has become one with the human reality. He is a full-blown, ground-level participant. It is about payment: Jesus pays in full. It is not that Jesus was deployed by God the Father to twist his own arm and buy off divine justice. Such talk masks a deep reality that confronts us in everyday lives, that when something happens it needs to be addressed and dealt with rather than be glossed over. Far more than a school or a government that issues rules and laws, God has to act. He has acted by identifying with us so fully in the person of Jesus, taking our place as one of us, paying for all our sins. We say to our times, 'God loves you and is willing to forgive you all your sin!'

The identification principle connects profoundly with the idea of the cross as being about the value of personhood and also debt. How could this throw light on the meaning of the death of Christ?

*'That which He has not assumed He has not healed . . .
What He was, He laid aside; what He was not, He assumed.
He takes upon Himself the poverty of my flesh so that I may
receive the riches of His divinity . . . Let us become like Christ,
since Christ became like us. He assumed the worse that
He might give us the better; He became poor that we
through His poverty might be rich.'*
Gregory of Nazianzus in the fourth century[1]

10

Trading places:
identification and exchange

Hebrews and visual aids

The letter to Hebrew Christians seems strange to post-Christian ears with all its talk of sacrifice, high priests, the blood of bulls and lambs. Yet it is teaching an object lesson, a visual aid making one central point: 'without the shedding of blood there is no forgiveness' (Hebrews 9:22). The writer has lived through those exciting changeover times, for Jesus, who had so recently lived among them, had passed through the heavens (4:14). Everything had changed. 'But now he has appeared once for all at the end of the ages to do away with sin by the sacrifice of himself' (9:26).

Until very recently, there passed a continual succession of priests and sacrifices to make atonement for this person and that sin. But then God sacrificed himself for the human race. It was a one-off; it was stupendous, and it was enough. In one single act, any other sacrifice is rendered redundant.

Jesus had appeared as a human being. His purpose, the writer says, was to do away with sins and to wash the slate clean. What qualified Jesus to become a sacrifice? If he chose to save us and needed to be in human form to make it happen, could he not have beamed down in human form at the age of thirty and then gone through the ordeal he set himself if there really was no alternative? Surely God could have sent an angel to fulfil the messy, murky task of redeeming human lives?

Hebrews makes the answers plain. It could not have been an angel. It had to be a human like us. But no-one could be the Saviour of humanity. Jesus, though, was uniquely qualified. In the infinite realm, there is someone who can represent us and who has acted for us. 'The point of what we are saying is this: We do have such a high priest, who sat down at the right hand of the throne of the Majesty in heaven' (Hebrews 8:1). Jesus became like a high priest in the Old Testament. A priest was someone who interceded with God for others, a go-between. A high priest was someone who represented a whole nation and who was called to do the job (5:1). You couldn't have just anyone stepping forward thinking that their self-sacrifice would achieve this.

Because Jesus was God and he was human, he could save humanity. He was high priest. But Jesus was also the sacrifice. Clearly, this is a vital difference. The high priest was not of course his own sacrifice but handled state sacrifices as the representative person. Hebrews argues that Jesus was both priest and sacrifice: 'He did not enter by means of the blood of goats and calves; but he entered the Most Holy Place once for all by his own blood, having obtained eternal redemption' (9:12).

The identification of God with humanity gives us our message. It is a message that the letter to the Hebrew Christians draws out, that God joined the human race to cancel the past and forgive our sin, to defeat the dark powers that haunt human existence, to stand in solidarity with us as our brother and to represent humanity before God. All these aspects of the death of Christ are important. Somehow, we have to connect this message with the wistfulness of the world.

That ties in with our experience. Those who have been through something similar are able to enter into our suffering. You do not need to have gone through exactly the same problem. Everyone has a unique set of experiences and motivations. From his insider status out of the lived experience of a marginalized community, Jesus experienced every state of humanity at ground level.

Without the atoning death of Jesus, there is nowhere to go with our wrongdoing, nowhere to transfer it to. This was the hidden and future promise in the story of the scapegoat in Old Testament times. The high priest laid hands on a goat that was then sent away into the wilderness while a second goat was slain. Jesus is the scapegoat. His death is a sacrifice that will take any sin that is sincerely acknowledged and transfer it to him. And he will take it, and take it away.

The cross as payment and exchange

From the pain and stain of the blood-soaked pathway of identification, what light can be thrown on a perplexing problem that has both drawn and repelled across the years? A key verse is this: 'God made him who had no sin to be sin for us, so that *in him* we might become the righteousness of God' (2 Corinthians 5:21).

This is a pivotal statement. It is not just judicial. It is about identification and transfer, or exchange. As twentieth-century writers emphasized, in Paul's thought there are two sets of terms that speak of transfer. One is about **participation** (from one state to another); the other is **judicial** (emphasizing guilt that is then compensated for). With the first, the focus is on being 'in Christ' such that being in his position through mutual identification enables us to switch our state. With the second, 'Christ dying for us' does the heavy lifting and we have forgiveness. These are different things, not contradictory. Bringing them together throws light on the flow of thought in Romans, where Paul moves from unearned righteousness straight into identification with death and Easter. How can forgiveness and participation in the cross and resurrection be somehow separate? They are not.

In the second letter to the Corinthians, Paul's statement here follows straight on from God's appeal to be reconciled. Aggrieved parties need reconciliation. Broken relationships require reconciliation.

The identification principle took Jesus deeply into the human condition. He lives our life, stands in solidarity with us in our weakness and with the victims in their pain. But he also takes our place, numbered as one of the transgressors. Jesus stood in the place of sinners as a sinning man in order that the sinning man and woman might be in a different state – acceptance with God.

In this book, our theme of the identification principle has been combined with that of value and worth. Humanity has immense value; people have worth because of the dignity with which they have been invested. Made in God's image, the value of the human soul stands out in reflected glory. Yet constantly we see the degradation of humanity. God should be honoured as the central sun.

In personal or social relationships, if people are devalued, some form of redress or compensation is always sought. They are valuable; that worth deserves to be respected when it is breached. When personal beings are rubbished, something needs to be done or said to put it right. It is akin to payment. Sin sets up an obligation that can only be met by means of transfer. It is not a monetary transaction but a symbolic one. Sin needs paying for as persons have immense value. The identification principle can apply very fruitfully to Jesus paying the price. The one who stands in solidarity with us meets it.

How does looking through that lens help us understand the cross? Here are five steps to walk up:

1. Sin violates sacredness – it devalues other people and dishonours God.
2. Some kind of payment is needed to acknowledge that this matters. Everyday interpersonal tensions demonstrate it. Impaired relationships require reconciliation and compensation.
3. In solidarity with humanity, Jesus steps in as divinely appointed representative to make a one-off payment for our indebtedness. He identifies as 'one of us'. Solidarity is the key.
4. At the cross Jesus absorbs both what people do to us and what we do to others. He pays the price.
5. An exchange is made in our state whereby human beings can be reconciled and participate in the standing and spirit of Christ. This is a complete reversal of our lack of worth.

Sin violates sacredness – it devalues other people and dishonours God.
Yes, we are made in God's image, made just a little lower than angels. We have high status. Yet sinfulness brings a marring of that image. Instead of honouring God and honouring the value of humanity, we devalue left, right and centre, and are in turn devalued by others. Personhood is sacred. Biblical times were framed by an honour culture. Promoting the honour of the

person, the family or the clan was vital. The dark side of honour was shame. For the most part we no longer live in a culture where social honour drives human behaviour. We do, though, live in a society that is conscious that people have value or not. Humanity devalues other people and devalues God. It is the essence of sinful actions that they violate the sacredness inherent in humanity. People have a value and a worth that can be infringed and assaulted. We become unworthy when we go against God, cease to honour him and fail to respect others. Christian hymnody and liturgy are replete with merit and de-merit, of unworthiness before God. We have lack of worth. It is not that God sees us as 'worthless' (though we may see ourselves in that way). Sinfulness sets up a deficit.

Blind to our blind spots, we fail to trace the wolf to its lair. Human sinfulness is not just about individuals doing the sort of evil that we recognize, it is perpetrated and sustained through cultures and systems that run our lives unseen.

Some kind of payment is needed to acknowledge that this matters. Everyday interpersonal tensions demonstrate it. Impaired relationships require reconciliation and compensation.

Someone is rubbished. Their value is walked all over. Compensation or recompense is called for by way of response. Opponents of any kind of idea of payment are simply not being true to life. In everyday life we find that letting someone down or hurting someone matters. 'You will pay for this' is an instinctive response, either spoken or unspoken. This is not tribal or antiquated but a fact of psychological life. Either we make others pay in some way or we demand payment from ourselves. It is called guilt. We go cool with those who annoy us. We cut people up on the road. The value of persons means that infringement sets up a deficit. Something happens that can only be discounted at the expense of denial of the value that someone has. If a group of local adolescents trash my garden, they are not trashing me directly, let alone God. Yet if they compound the action and fail to acknowledge that this is an issue, they are definitely walking over me, as well as the flower beds. What is needed is not just reparation but recognition. The teenage boys are devaluing me as a moral being worthy of recognition. They are saying in effect, 'Like your garden, you are worthless.'

The same people who downplay the death of Christ as an atoning sacrifice would presumably smile in generosity of spirit if you apologized for accidently treading on their toes. But if you were to accidently tread on someone's toes and didn't say sorry, anyone would feel indignant.

We have a strong antenna for injustice – especially when it has been done to us. If slandered, we demand compensation. Civil and criminal law alike revolve around the idea of payment to us or a debt to society, of addressing wrongdoing.

Because of the role that honour and disrespect play in human dynamics, experiencing devaluation needs compensating for. There is now a deficit. Some sort of marketplace is set up. A strong impulse with human violence is 'I have been devalued and disrespected so I will take it from you'. The only way I can regain value and honour is to scrape it from you. I need recompense and will take it.

When we experience being written off or rubbished, something has been breached in our depths. It is core material, primal wounding. It evokes a primal cry of 'I'm worth more than that!' Indebtedness arises. Someone must pay. The same desecration that has been inflicted on us must be visited upon others. Recompense will ensure that my depleted bank account is restored. This is what makes forgiveness hard work. 'Forgive us our debt' is a way of articulating the need to cover the aggrieving by the aggrieved. Atonement theology is usually expressed in terms of the law courts, sacrificial language or that of the slave market and its overtones of redemption. But the demand for compensation is utterly true to life. It pursues us across the years. A judge sentencing an offender will work with a scale of tariffs. We have to pay; we always have to pay. Impaired relationships require reconciliation and compensation, restitution or even prison (depending on the seriousness).

But does God need placating? Surely yes, for the same reason that humans do. God is involved in this process. In the nexus of human actions that devalue others and deny their worth, he is a major player. This takes place at two levels. First, he is guarantor and source of the value of personhood. Second, he is not acknowledged. Our times have witnessed a monumental failure to take God seriously. The impetus to make up the deficit towards God must be relieved, the debt paid.

In solidarity with humanity, Jesus steps in as divinely appointed representative to make a one-off payment for our indebtedness. He identifies as 'one of us'. Solidarity is the key.
All this can sound as if it is purely a matter of legalities or payment, inappropriate to a God of love. In reality, it is the relations between humanity and God and between people that are at stake. In our human experience, the demand for compensation is only a way of describing those relations and what happens when they are broken. We have failed to grasp the relevance of the cross.

The identification principle took Jesus all the way to Calvary where he was crucified one Friday morning. Identification is the way to understand it. At the cross, Jesus is not standing in the position of an outsider. He has insider status. He is one of us! The crude, unreflective version of atonement that has God say 'I must punish, who can I punish?', before Jesus kindly steps in and pays the price, is wide of the mark.

Jesus does pay the price for our sin but does so from within as a fully paid-up member of humanity.

Solidarity is a tricky issue in contemporary society. Who speaks for whom? Who has legitimacy and the right to speak for a particular social group? Jesus identifies with us in full, thus affirming our human worth, but also taking on himself the sin and violence. He was probably a working man, but he was definitely Jewish.

Who was this one who lives, who spoke as he did, died and rose again? Can Jesus speak for the women of Africa or Afghanistan? Can Jesus act as the representative of humanity, and does such an entity even exist? Talk of Jesus Christ being a federal head, rather like a modern-day president, is less relevant today than brotherhood and sisterhood.

Jesus makes a one-off representative payment. The cross was fundamentally necessary, to pay for the wrong actions, wrong words and wrong attitudes that have accumulated on our track record, because we have devalued others and dishonoured God. The cross is the speeding fine being paid for, the penalty points on the licence being erased. It is compensation paid to the victim of injustice, whether by financial award or by sentencing of the perpetrator. Is that what our sinning has done? Only the cross can save us because it pays for the damage. What a vast amount was needed in compensation to be a payment on a global scale! Jesus stands shoulder to shoulder with the innocent and the guilty and pays a price for us. The love is beyond contemplation.

At the cross Jesus absorbs both what people do to us and what we do to others. He pays the price. An exchange is made in our state whereby human beings can be reconciled and participate in the standing and spirit of Christ. This is a complete reversal of our lack of worth.

Looking at the cross through the lens of Jesus paying the price for our sins is instructive. The second letter to the Corinthians 5:21 speaks of an exchange in our state, rooted in impaired relationships and the need for reconciliation. The heart of the atoning sacrifice of Jesus is that when sin occurs, something has happened that needs to be addressed. It cannot be 'un-happened' and time doesn't erode it away. And that brings us to the relationship of 'Christ-for-us' and 'we-in-Christ' – two conceptions that are different but that we cannot separate. The corporate idea is bound up with the substitutionary one. Paul, in Romans 5:12 onwards, links the corporate idea of being in Adam to Jesus' death for us.[2]

This central part of Christ's identification with us meets our need because it is true to life. When we do wrong, something has just taken place that it would be wrong to ignore. Someone must pay. Indebtedness inevitably arises. 'Dying in our place' (the just for the unjust) sets up a kind of symbolic exchange, a transfer of value akin to what happens in everyday transactions when we purchase something. Similarly, when Jesus offered to pay for the damage as the human representative, it sets up an exchange – the righteous for the unrighteous; his life for ours, his riches for our poverty. He switches states. It enables us to be reconciled to God and enter a new humanity embodied by Jesus. At the heart of the atonement is exchange. It brings together two ideas in fruitful combination:

1. the value and worth of personhood
2. the identification principle.

Identification is at the heart of incarnation. The embrace of the human by the divine is fundamental to the incarnation and represents an affirmation of it. The incarnation does justice to the material side of our existence. It gives value to the material order. In embracing the life that people live, God assigns importance to the human body, the body that was torn apart by violence to pay the price.

A new state

'But now . . .' (Romans 3:21) – the two most dynamic words in the New Testament. It is central to Paul's philosophy of history, to the plan of salvation that split history in two.

The sin debt was *'Paid in full'*. His righteousness has been credited to our account. We owed a debt we could never pay. Jesus paid it in full. *Tetelestai* (the Greek word in John 19:30) says this, as it did in the days of Jesus, when a promissory note was paid. Property could not be translated into ownership unless dated and signed, and *tetelestai* written by a scribe across the deed. A debt that was paid off had *tetelestai* written on a certificate of debt to show it was 'Paid in full'.[3]

Sometimes the atoning death of Jesus can be presented in a way that a blood sacrifice was needed to persuade God to be forgiving. But Jesus and the Father are one. Calvary is God himself standing in full identification with humanity and taking our place. Jesus does not persuade a reluctant Father to forgive. Because of Jesus accomplishing the great work of redeeming humanity, we are now *'in him'*. Christ dying *for* us could mean 'in our favour' and not just 'in our place'. But 2 Corinthians 5:21, and other texts, point to the death of Christ through substitution: 'If anyone is in Christ, there is a new creation' (2 Corinthians 5:17, NRSV). It is reconciled humanity, flushed with new power, new orientation, new perspective and, above all, new relationship. The emphasis on 'reconciliation' highlights Paul's insight that we are profoundly relational, not isolated solitaries. Paul describes the contrast in states and positions: 'For you know the grace of our Lord Jesus Christ, that though he was rich, yet for your sakes he became poor, so that you through his poverty might become rich' (2 Corinthians 8:9).

The exchanged life has always been central to Christian thought. Twentieth-century writers noticed the emphasis Paul placed on being 'in Christ', on participation in his life and his standing. The focus for this is the identification principle. Jesus took our position, which becomes the means by which we can enter his. Justification is often interpreted in terms of God accepting us because he is kind and gracious. The emphasis rather is that a swap takes place. Through faith in Christ, righteousness is given to us in place of our filthy rags. It is about position. Being an authentic part of the old humanity by reason of his natural life, Jesus opens up to us the means of being included in the new humanity.

Justification by faith is a tremendously powerful idea. Long before its rediscovery at the Reformation, it was central to Paul's message in the earliest Christian writing ever – the letter to the Galatians. This is not just, as the new perspective on Paul has it, a change of status whereby we believe in Christ and become part of God's people. It is a change of state and position before God, a transfer and transition from sin to righteousness arising from Jesus' total identification. Our position changes by dint of the identification of Christ with us. Because of who he was and is, there is a new humanity that emerges on the other side of the inclusive cross. His righteousness is credited to our account, as it were. As in a ledger, the balance of the books is completely changed. Forgiveness and remission results in a cancelling of the indebtedness (Romans 4:9). There is a positive side of the ledger. The exchange results in positive merit flooding our account. Righteousness is credited to us. Right standing is given to us. We are granted a secure place of acceptance with the Father.

Divine forgiveness results in human beings being able to forgive each other. This is hard work because it feels like a betrayal of the person who was wronged. At the violent cross, forgiveness can be exercised precisely because Jesus upholds and respects the value of the victims of violence. He was one. It leads to disarming the weapons. This takes place as we are included in him, within the sphere and impact of the death of Christ. It is why being 'in Christ' is also such a powerful idea but integral to a transfer of state. 'If we have been united with him like this in his death, we will certainly also be united with him in his resurrection' (Romans 6:5).

Resurrection

The cross is a stunning turning of the tables on the powers of darkness (who thought they had won their greatest victory in killing the God-man). It was an instant turnaround against those who believed that they had finished with Jesus and rid themselves of this man who was both the walking embodiment of goodness and a thorough nuisance. The Gospels do not record the personal reactions of Pilate, Herod and Caiaphas – three major players who believed they had stopped the dangerous talk of another king and another kingdom. But their work was to be completely undone.

The destruction of a human life that they had envisaged was turned from defeat into sudden victory because the life they thought they had destroyed was more than human. 'Having disarmed the powers and authorities, [Jesus] made a public spectacle of them, triumphing over them by the cross' (Colossians 2:15). The death of Jesus was the death knell of the devil and a trumpet sounding the ultimate defeat of the dark powers. An enormous stone couldn't stop him, the military guard couldn't stop him, death couldn't hold him, and Satan could only watch incredulous.

It is this complete reversal on Easter Sunday morning that provides potent truth to help the sinful and the hurting. Jesus identified with trapped humanity, to fight our battles. Though Jesus went down into defeat, he trusted God for the reversal, as Psalm 16 has it. Good Friday concluded with doom and gloom, the extinguishing of hope and the death of light. Watch for the third day! The stone was rolled away by powerful, divine hands. All that sealed Jesus into coldness of death was replaced by the surprising victory of God. Confident that Jesus had defeated the dark powers that bound the human race, the first Christians went everywhere to sound the ultimate defeat of sin, despair, death and the devil. The Adam humanity had just been declared 'old', for a new Christ humanity was beginning to be abroad on the earth.

In the countless situations in our world where it seems evil has triumphed, the victory of Christ and God's great act of reversal proclaims that evil will be defeated. Death does not have the last word. It looked as if the result was certain, but there was extra time and a surprise victory. God has the last laugh, and those who tune their ears to Calvary can begin to hear it. The victory of God can be proclaimed in the teeth of those same dark powers that appeared to have won. Those bound by sin, despair, death and evil can be free if they believe the announcement and emerge from their prison. 'Say to the captives, "Come out," and to those in darkness, '"Be free!"'' (Isaiah 49:9).

Being included in the new humanity that Jesus now identifies with is dynamic. The best guide to this is Romans, with its paeon of praise to the resurrected life. 'There is therefore now no condemnation for those who are in

Christ Jesus . . . you are not in the flesh; you are in the Spirit' (Romans 8:1, 9, NRSV). Paul moves in a series of filmstrips to outline the dynamic of the new humanity. Through the death and resurrection, where incorporation takes place and the great transfer is made, believers have a new status, a new relationship, a new freedom and a new power. This is the Pauline philosophy of history, for it shows how God intervened in the face of the creeping paralysis in the moral life of humanity. The way we were has dramatically shifted. There is a 'no longer', though also a 'not yet', in the story of salvation.

The church in Ephesus received less systematic exposition on what participation means, but it did learn this upward trajectory: 'Because of his great love for us, God, who is rich in mercy, made us alive with Christ even when we were dead in transgressions – it is by grace you have been saved. And God raised us up with Christ and seated us with him in the heavenly realms in Christ Jesus' (Ephesians 2:4–6).

To use metaphors of space and place, the identification principle took Jesus down to being in human form, down into death and then up, up to resurrection and the highest pinnacle of all (Philippians 2:7–11). Those who go beyond merely being part of a common humanity and are actively joined to Christ through his death and resurrection realize that there is someone in the heavenly realms who resembles us. His humanity and ours has been taken up and adopted by God for ever!

Part Two

Being incarnational:
what is to be done?

11

Prayer and pathos:
incarnation and intercession

Keeping God company

On this part of our journey, we begin to probe what it means for our times to be incarnational once again, to re-engage. Jesus did not inoculate himself against the sufferings of his fellows. In such full-immersion baptism, he crossed boundaries to reach out to women, to children, to the undervalued and to social lepers. The pathway Jesus chose to restore humanity was a difficult road to take. He got in there with us; a fully paid-up member of the humanity he had lovingly fashioned.

Prayer is a kaleidoscope of possibility. Surpassing all the doctorates from all the best universities, keeping God company is the highest learning that humans can ever rise to, for it responds to the descent of God and the profound identification with our humanity that left us a path to walk in.

There are many calls and demands on our time and we cannot respond to every call and every demand. The need to spend well resources of time, energy and finances God has entrusted us with is vital to the skill of living. One of those calls is personal time. The model of Jesus' identification is our guide. Jesus committed himself to investing in close relationships; at least half his ministry was spent with his immediate disciples. And Jesus was known for time spent alone. Time was something that he budgeted carefully, and from a busy ministry he carved out prayer. We don't see in the Gospels a portrait of a need-driven man but someone who defined his purpose, who knew what he was up to and what he should be doing in any situation. Being clear about our objectives – and letting those be shaped by the Word of God and prayer – will liberate us to be purpose-driven in a need-driven world.

'I only do the things my Father shows me' was the guiding principle of how the identification of Jesus worked out in his ministry. He was not rushed off his feet in response to human need but responded knowing what he should be doing. Of course there were times when his humanity must have cried out for respite. He sits down at a well for refreshment on a journey while his disciples were visiting the local supermarket. A woman comes up and Jesus asks her for a drink. He is tired, hot and dry, but immediately another ministry opportunity stares at Jesus (John 4). Or he retreats to a lonely spot where he can pause for breath. But it was not to be. The crowds are pursuing. Though stretched and longing for relief, Jesus realizes something. It is the crowd who are harassed and pushed every which way by life. It is borne in upon Jesus that he cannot respond to every situation. There must be more, plenty more who will come to labour in the harvest of the world. Even Jesus in his ministry is limited. While he was in Galilee, he could not be in Judea.

The cross was the culmination of this extraordinary act of identification, but it was not the destination. For the identification principle took Jesus beyond death into life and back into the Father's presence. Bearing still the scars of his experiences, with the marks of the cross fresh upon him, Jesus engages in a ministry of intercession. This is what that brief immersion into the human condition was leading up to.

For a brief moment, God joined us. He acquired human experience and stood in empathetic solidarity with our suffering and died in our place. There is no hard distinction between 'God with us' and 'God for us'. The incarnation led to atonement; the latter is grounded in the former. It was an awesome transfer of value and standing; the just for the unjust, the worthy one for the unworthy.

Was this incandescent moment of incarnation a temporary dive into the grubby human condition, to see what it was like for a while and leave behind a deposit of salvation that can be drawn upon in his absence? Biblical material replies with a resounding 'No'. Jesus, the focal point of divine identification with our humanity, returned to become our advocate. Humanity has a representative with the ultimate power that rules the universe.

Not every nation will have permanent representatives everywhere. We are God's ambassadors (2 Corinthians 5:20), as if God were making his personal continuing appeal to humanity through us, a flawed mouthpiece. We have an ambassador with God, a permanent representative in the infinite realm. There is an advocate interceding for us, liberating and strengthening our lives and urging us forward to every good endeavour.

Anyone who has gone abroad and left vital concerns in the hands of a solicitor or agent understands the importance of an advocate you can trust. Facing a tribunal or a difficult matter that has arisen, you need someone working for you who will give you confidence.

> My dear children, I write this to you so that you will not sin.
> But if anybody does sin, we have one who speaks to the Father
> in our defence – Jesus Christ, the Righteous One. He is the
> atoning sacrifice for our sins, and not only ours but also for
> the sins of the whole world. (1 John 2:1–2)

Having lived among us and died for our sins, Jesus defends
our true interests (but not just those that underpin comfort
and happiness!).

Jesus has entered into a new phase of his ministry, interceding
for us and extending the impact of his atoning sacrifice deep
into the human situation. Having come to our level and
ascended the ladder again, the Son has not yet completed the
assignment. Human experience and the astounding death for
others did but qualify him to practise at the bar of God as the
advocate for a world gone wrong. The new phase of his ministry
is permanent. Jesus Christ is locked into the human race. There
is an ongoing task of ministry to a broken world that shows
deep commitment. Incarnation was not a phase he went
through or a temporary transaction. He sought a permanent
relationship, embedded in the identification principle.

Nowhere is this better illustrated than in the book of Hebrews.

Jesus the intercessor

The priests in the Old Testament were mediators, representing
people before God and bringing their sacrifice. And they were
human, standing on behalf of frail humanity. There was a high
priest, who did not just represent individual people, he represented the nation.

> Every high priest is selected from among men and is appointed
> to represent them in matters related to God, to offer gifts and

sacrifices for sins. He is able to deal gently with those who are
ignorant and are going astray, since he himself is subject to
weakness. (Hebrews 5:1–2)

The writer goes on to speak of the way Jesus agonized as he
prepared to sacrifice himself for the sins of the world: 'During
the days of Jesus' life on earth, he offered up prayers and
petitions with loud cries and tears to the one who could save
him from death, and he was heard because of his reverent
submission' (Hebrews 5:7). This was intercessory pathos; raw,
rugged emotion.

In the identification of Jesus with our humanity, his life and
death were of a single piece. Hebrews 9:14 will go on to affirm
that only by the shedding of blood is there forgiveness –
something happens in human sinfulness that has to be
addressed; there is a price to be paid. But it was the humanity
of Jesus, with that full range of experiences, that qualified him
to act as a sacrifice for the sins of the world.

This is the continuity between the death and life of Jesus.
'Although he was a son, he learned obedience from what he
suffered and, once made perfect, he became the source of
eternal salvation for all who obey him and was designated by
God to be high priest in the order of Melchizedek' (Hebrews
5:8–10). 'He was a son . . . he learned . . . he became . . . and
was designated . . .' The order is surely significant. It was not
just becoming human that enabled Jesus to be the world
Saviour. Endurance and suffering qualified Jesus to stand on
behalf of frail, sinful humanity – one in frailty, though not in
personal sin (5:7). The high priest had to offer sacrifice for his
own sins as well as the sins of the people (5:3). Not so Jesus.

It is impressive that the writer should place such an emphasis
on Jesus acting as a high priest when he certainly did not come
from a priestly family and had no official connection whatever

with official religion. 'No-one from that tribe has ever served at the altar. For it is clear that our Lord descended from Judah, and in regard to that tribe Moses said nothing about priests' (Hebrews 7:13–14).

Step by step the solidarity of Jesus with our humanity took him into intercession. His deep identification with the human race cannot be separated from the way he stands on our behalf now. The intercession of Christ means the identification continues to this day in an unbroken thread and a seamless robe. 'Because Jesus lives for ever, he has a permanent priesthood. Therefore he is able to save completely those who come to God through him, because he always lives to intercede for them' (Hebrews 7:24–25).

Now Jesus has embarked upon a new phase of his ministry – the ministry of intercession. The thirty-three-year life and the six-hour crucifixion were a preparation for what was to come. A deep and profound identification with humanity in life and death had provided the means to save anyone – the author of salvation, as Hebrews 5:10 declares (author: Greek *aitios* – the cause).

In ancient Israel, the high priests prepared themselves by performing all their functions and tasks in the right order. With the blood of the sacrifice in their hands, once a year they entered the holy place, a temple made with hands, to plead with God to cleanse the nation. An annual drama was re-enacted, the high priest fearing for his life as he crept behind the curtain into the presence of God. And on his cloak, close to his palpitating heart were the insignia of the twelve tribes.

In striking imagery, Jesus sat down in the presence of God, having obtained human redemption: the mission completed, the task fulfilled. High Priests would have to leave the inner sanctuary as soon as their ministry was completed, returning the following year. Jesus sat down; there was no need to leave or to return. 'After he had provided purification for sins, he sat down at the right hand of the Majesty in heaven' (Hebrews 1:3); 'When this priest had offered for all time one sacrifice for sins, he sat down at the right hand of God' (10:12); 'Jesus . . . sat down at the right hand of the throne of God' (12:2).

The conclusion in Hebrews is that the Son of God continues to identify with humanity. His identification did not cease on returning to the infinite realm. There is someone who resembles us. His earthly life provided the basis for a sacrifice of unlimited power; the self-sacrifice of Jesus became a doorway into the next phase of his ministry. The Son of God has become an intercessor. His earthly life was but a brief interval, the death of Christ the drama of a moment. But the intercessory ministry has been continuing for two thousand years. It was all so Jesus could have something to plead and dispense the new covenant to all who come to God through him. Jesus was divinely accredited by God to speak for the human race. In the great dispute God had with humanity, he supplied the mediator. Jesus our intermediary was one of us, not standing above the fray but fully aware of the complexity and struggle of being human. Being also God, he does what no other can: he unites both parties in himself and brings both together. And still he remains faithful and committed to this ministry, bearing our cause near to his heart as the High Priest of Israel.

How do you plead?

To be most helpful to the Christian church, theology has to engage with countless issues that are pressing and urgent. It must throw light on what we do and point the way forward.

The theology of intercessory prayer is a vital issue to understand and grasp, for with it lies the future success and effectiveness of the church. Upon the issue of in-depth prayer, an atlas burden of urgency is resting.

Intercession, standing on behalf of some people, is effective when we are identifying with them and taking their place. This is why God answers that prayer. It seems illegal and invalid. Why on earth should some people be blessed, out of all the thousands around them, just because someone has been praying for them? Does the intercession of another override their own freedom?

Perhaps God treats it as if a person has been praying on his or her own account.

Intercession, prayer for others, is the process by which we stand between God, who has the answer, and a situation of human need. Intercession is 'an act of pleading for another'. It comes from two Latin words – *inter* (between) and *cedere* (to go). An intercessor is a go-between. A mother who intercedes with a dad or a headteacher is a go-between, acting on behalf of her anxious child who has got into trouble. A mediator in a troubled marriage is a peacemaker, bringing both parties together, as is a mediator in an industrial or international conflict. The mediation of Jesus cannot be separated from his intercession. Intercession is based on identification. Jesus identifying with us was an act of intercession that involved his whole life and death. The pastoral epistles refer to the mediation of Jesus Christ and intercession in the same breath (1 Timothy 2:1–6).

> I revealed myself to those who did not ask for me; I was found
> by those who did not seek me. To a nation that did not call
> on my name, I said, 'Here am I, here am I.' All day long I have
> held out my hands to an obstinate people. (Isaiah 65:1–2)

'I was found by those who did not seek me.' Why? Because those who did know God asked. Does this throw any light on the mystery of prayer and how God can justly answer prayer from someone who isn't even praying? We are praying, but it is as if they are praying. We are standing in their place.

It is because we are standing on their behalf. We are pleading with God, but as we identify with that person and take their place, it is as if they are praying for themselves. Intercession works by virtue of identification.

It is not enough to grasp in a theoretical way that identification is the basis of intercession. The way Jesus did not stand aloof from humanity but got deeply and fervently involved cannot be allowed to remain as an interesting proposition. So how do you plead? 'During the days of Jesus' life on earth, he offered up prayers and petitions with loud cries' (Hebrews 5:7). Passion and pathos always get through.

It needs the intercession of God's people to become engaged and involved and to apply that to a given situation, a soul or a city under the domination of dark powers. Where that does not happen, the connection is not made and compassion-based power does not run into the situation, the soul or the city.

There is nothing left. We have to get on our knees. The pattern of Jesus' intercession for the world is threaded with fervour and passion to go and make connection. The same must be true of our intercession: involved intercession must take the form of passionate pleading. Why should God see someone else as he hears our prayer unless we are involved and engaged? By definition, the level of intercession that breaks through will not be love on the sidelines. It will be a love that shares a person's future and destiny as if it were our own. We will be praying as if we were that person. Dispassionate intercession is a contradiction in terms.

158 | PRAYER AND PATHOS

Every revival in history has been birthed in intercession, and every ministry that has engraved God on other lives is forged in its flame. Such intercession marks the spirit of Paul in that most vital part of his letter to the Romans:

> I am speaking the truth in Christ – I am not lying; my conscience confirms it by the Holy Spirit – I have great sorrow and unceasing anguish in my heart. For I could wish that I myself were accursed and cut off from Christ for the sake of my own people, my kindred according to the flesh. (Romans 9:1–3, NRSV)

This is the man who has written sublime teaching of our position in Christ and the certainty of our final salvation. This is the man who has traced in the sands of history the purposes of God. This is the man who knows of the love of God from which nothing can separate and nothing come between. He speaks of a creation groaning in the pangs of childbirth and, in sympathy with that, we who are the first fruits of the Spirit also share in creation's sigh (Romans 8:23). He has also spoken of the way the Spirit intercedes within the children of God, 'with groans that words cannot express' (8:26). And he has described how Christ is at the right hand of God and 'is also interceding for us' (8:34).

A groaning creation, a passionate Spirit within us, a Christ at the seat of power – this is the circuit he makes. But for the sake of those for whom he prays, it is a circuit he is prepared to break in his own case if forfeiting his salvation will lead to the conversion of his people. Paul knows his Lord did no less for him, taking the place of a sinning world and allowing judgment to fall upon him personally. This is the spirit of identification. Empathetic, concerned, passionate identification, taking the place of someone else or a whole group of people – such was the spirit of Jesus, of Daniel and of Paul.

Excursion – One pleading man

One of the heroes of intercession is a man who is virtually unknown today, though his surname lives on in the Salvation Army. His life and service for God exemplify the deep and profound identification with the cause and people of God that results in passionate pleading. He was a circuit-maker.[1]

William Bramwell, born in 1759, became a preacher in the glow of second-generation Methodism. In the year John Wesley died, Bramwell was appointed superintendent of a circuit centred on the town of Dewsbury. The circuit had experienced division after its trustees had separated from Wesley. The founder of Methodism wrote a booklet about the incident entitled *The case of the Dewsbury House recommended to the consideration of the people called Methodists.*

Because of the division, Bramwell saw little fruit in the first year of his labours. His response was to give himself to constant prayer for the outpouring of the Holy Spirit. He invited people to pray with him at 5 o'clock every morning. Then came Ann Cutler. It was her regular practice to spend the night hours between 3 and 4 o'clock to plead with God for revival. By 4 o'clock, Bramwell was taking up the cause and was also praying fervently.

> As I was praying in my room, I received an answer from God in a particular way and had the revival discovered to me in its manner and effects. I had no more doubt. All my grief was gone. I could say, the Lord will come – I know He will come and that suddenly.

It happened just as he saw. The fire fell and began to spread. The next quarter, a hundred new members were added to the Methodist Society.

It was the same story everywhere Bramwell laboured. From Dewsbury, he was appointed to nearby Birstal. The record continues:

> Mr Bramwell, on entering this circuit, gave himself much
> to prayer and sometimes spent whole nights in this exercise.
> At the lovefeast on Christmas Day, the Lord poured out His
> Spirit in a very remarkable manner. Many persons were deeply
> awakened and upwards of fifty people obtained forgiveness
> of their sins. From this time, opposition ceased; preachers and
> leaders were united in the work.[2]

Some 600 people were brought to Christ during his time there.

In 1795 he was in Sheffield, where a spiritual revival was already taking place in the city. Around the circuit, however, it was a different story. 'I cannot yet find *one pleading man*,' he wrote. 'There are many good people but I have found no wrestlers with God.' His own spirit caught. He began to meet with a small group, a Methodist band that met early in the morning once a week. Soon,

> the embers of love were rekindled all around, and when he
> visited the Societies, he found them striving together for the
> furtherance of the gospel; opposition was broken down,
> lukewarmness disappeared, a holy union prevailed and the
> work of God in the town and country broke out into a flame
> of life and power.

About 1,500 people were added to the Methodist classes in his three years of labour at Sheffield. 'I never witnessed in any other man such a burning love to God and man,' wrote someone there who became a friend. 'This servant of God is owned and succeeded of God wherever he goes. I have been drinking larger draughts of the love of God. I want to be filled, actuated and inflamed with this continually.'

The secret of Bramwell's stirring ministry was his entire reliance on the cooperation of the Holy Spirit. He walked in the spirit of believing prayer, groaned for the lost and laboured intensely.

It was written of him that few men could enter more into the apostolic spirit exhibited in Paul: 'My little children, for whom I am again in the pain of childbirth until Christ is formed in you' (Galatians 4:19, NRSV). 'I have three weeks of agony,' wrote Bramwell upon entering the Hull circuit in 1804, 'but now see the Lord working.' 'I see souls saved,' he wrote later, 'but the work is not general . . . the flame of love and salvation is now breaking out on every side in Hull. I know we cannot fast and pray in vain.' From the house of a friend, no vessel could pass along the Humber river unseen. Here a first-floor room was available to William Bramwell where he could meet with God for days of fasting and communion. From 9 in the morning until 3 in the afternoon, this holy man of God burned with love for God and humanity and went out to see people won to a living faith.

Bramwell wanted others to catch the same spirit. 'O be a wonder in your circuit,' he wrote to young men in the ministry while he was at Sunderland,

a wonder in preaching and in zeal for the salvation of men.
O be a weighty man of God . . . there is now too much labour
to be popular . . . Let your end be always the salvation of men,
study this and you will achieve it, write all your sermons before
you preach them but do not write too much . . . let nothing but
souls brought to God satisfy you . . . strive to bring some home
to God in every sermon.

An eyewitness account at this time reports the impression that William Bramwell made on him. Even the way Bramwell gave out the hymn numbers spoke that here was a holy man of God.

> The gravity of his appearance in the pulpit, his powerful and pleading spirit in prayer when he seemed to commune with his Maker at the mercy-seat and then the bold, impassioned and energetic manner of his preaching, not only riveted my attention to his subject, but awakened in my heart such emotions as led me then and there to give myself to God. (The Revd Alexander Bell)

One letter written from Sunderland captures the spirit of passionate identification perhaps more than any other: 'O this heaven of God's presence, the opening into glory, this weeping over a lost world, this being willing to lay down your life for the church. God is all. O my soul. I feel its fire, its burning as I write. God grant the flame may spread, the glory shine.'

Being incarnational

This is the spirit of intercession, the spirit that is deeply involved, passionately committed to the salvation of humanity. Bramwell exhibited it and moved round his circuits like a flame of fire. Paul exhibited it when he groaned in birthpangs for the formation of Christ in the Galatian Christians. Daniel exemplified it when he identified with the Jewish people of his day and acknowledged 'we have sinned'. But towering above them all, Jesus embodied it when he lived and died and rose again in full and voluntary identification with humanity. He is the exemplar.

In the mould of the identification of Jesus, the spirit of intercession becomes clearest. His life and death was a prayer for the salvation of those around him. And he demonstrates why such intercession will be heard, that God will answer when we plead with emotion on behalf of others, showing that we are taking their place. Justly, legitimately, in truth, they are praying for themselves.

Uncomfortable though it is, most people out there think that God is irrelevant to their real needs. The life of the world and the life of the church flow in separate rivers. Old connections have been broken and the church should reconnect with the paradoxical new world we find ourselves in.

The call is there. It's always been there. It comes from a God who took into his very being our sin, our suffering and all our sorrows, absorbing it all without recoil, who looks on the crowded cities of the world and has compassion on them 'because they were harassed and helpless, like sheep without a shepherd' (Matthew 9:36). The owner of the harvest pleads still for labourers. Passionate identification moves us into relevant ministry to the post-Christian, post-millennial human situation, but this is only the first way of being incarnational we are looking at. The identification principle takes us further.

*'The Word became flesh and blood,
and moved into the neighbourhood.'*
(John 1:14, *The Message*)

12

The power of proclamation:
a new incarnational apologetic

Anointed solidarity

A confident church, bold in its message, is not bright and breezy. We are kept rooted by our own humanity. However, we are not just down to earth, of the earth, earthy. There is that within the church witnessing to Christ that is born from above and reaches to its source. Just as the old humanity represented the breath of God enlivening the man of earth (Genesis 2), the new humanity was generated by the Holy Spirit (Luke 1). This went beyond natural vitality and vigour. The Spirit of God was brooding, hovering, over the face of the deep once again. Having identified with natural humanity and dwelt in the ordinariness of life for many years, Jesus then comes forth and stands in the Jordan, so potent with meaning, so redolent of the nation's symbolism. He was not so very far from where Elijah goes to the left bank across waters that have parted for him and his apprentice. Elisha gives expression to a long-cherished aspiration, that he should have a double portion of his master's spirit before he is carried off (2 Kings 2:9). He is completely focused on this request to the point where he keeps his eyes on Elijah for as long as eyes allow. The mantle from the mentor falls and Elisha is clothed with power from on high. 'Where now is the LORD, the God of Elijah?' (2 Kings 2:14)

For a church intent on incarnational life, these are vital verses. Living the mission of Jesus requires not only solidarity but anointed solidarity. It was not enough that Jesus identified with humanity as he came for baptism; the Spirit must again hover over the waters. The man from Nazareth must become the anointed saviour, Jesus the Christ. As a representative man, Jesus must become a Word and Spirit man, filled with Spirit-power, promising power from on high to those who would follow (Luke 24:49). Jesus is clothed with a new authority that stuns everyone who comes into contact with its dynamic force. The anointing that Jesus experienced at his baptism is powerful accreditation. Now he can practise the craft of ministry. Cloaked with authority, the Spirit of God upon him produced transformative encounters among the people (elites weren't so impressed).

The summons is clear. It was anointing even Jesus needed to be receptive to. How far the experience was transformative, bringing Jesus into a new dimension, we cannot say. The Spirit is being linked to the role of God's servant. What that means for us has to do with authority. Something compelling and demanding attention was upon Jesus. Memory is fading in the modern church of generations past who, like William Bramwell, used to speak of such things. The need of the church today is unchanged; to serve its generation by the will of God and widen the transformative coverage of the gospel net. Presence alone is surely insufficient if we are to take our cue from Jesus. The routines of Nazareth where he lived the life of ordinary people and knew their psychodramas needed in time to be complemented by the anointing that gave him access to a realm beyond the purely human. The anointing was to do with spiritual authority that wrapped Jesus in a prophetic mantle that he embodied.

The good news did not arrive from a clear blue sky. John's was a voice in the desert, yet the voice was expressed in a living, breathing human. The Word that was the self-expression of God did not sound in disembodied fashion above the cacophony of words and the tumult of noise. It was embodied, embedded, in a particular person in time and place and space.

Incarnation was God's communication method. It still is. People will not hear a message unless it is embodied. 'The Word became flesh and moved into the neighbourhood.' They call it 'contextual'. For some, this calls for largely eschewing verbal evangelism in favour of the very specific work of 'place-making', and personal commitments to that locality. Renewing lost community is imperative.

For others, proclamation arising from conviction, especially biblical conviction, is what should be emphasized and indeed constitutes our only valid call. Social transformation is irrelevant. Enriching society in Jesus' name and preaching the good news about him go hand in hand. The Word that became human and moved into the neighbourhood was the self-expression of God that demands constant expression and re-articulation until such time as the church has done its work in the world.

Conviction politicians (the church equivalent)

The Christian church has a severe attack that is seriously damaging its health. I write this at a time when thousands in the UK and around the world are going down with influenza.

But the situation facing us is not a physical illness, though it results in ill-health and malaise. It is a crisis of confidence.

The authority question is a huge issue in today's world. Authoritarian regimes are on the rise again. On the one hand there is a bewildering tumult of noise. In a noisy marketplace of ideas, messages from advertisers and politicians crowd the air. Tweets are the birdsong of our time. Now it has been aroused, the social media hubbub will never be silenced.

'The Christian world is in a deep sleep,' said George Whitefield. 'I love those that thunder out the word!' Authentic conviction will always cut through and make a way for itself, to provoke thought and heart-searching (not dumbed-down messages in a world entertaining itself to sleep).

We forget what a weighty challenge the first missionaries of the cross faced as they sought to plant the flag of good news among the nations. In its early time, the spread of Christianity took place on unpromising soil. The good news was one message among many in the marketplace. Syncretistic paganism and mystery religions jostled in the arena with Greek deities and their Roman equivalents. The monotheistic space was already taken: first-century Jewish life and practice presented formidable antibodies against rival deviations. And yet the missionaries of Jesus set out to conquer the world. They did so, confident to the point of crazy conviction that God had drawn very close to the world just a few years previously and become part of it to save it. They were passionate people.

It is that conviction we need to recover without delay. When fused with passion, conviction is profound, deeply rooted and inspirational. It is also incarnational. It is also deeply biblical as, without it, conviction and confidence withers and we end up dumb. There is no witness to the incarnation other than that contained in Scripture. Through a process of mass discernment, an agreed canon took shape that gives us apostolic legitimacy through continuity.

Articulated through flesh and blood prophets, priests and kings, the biblical witness was clothed with their story and their persona. It comes to its decisive culmination in *the* embodiment of God. Now it begs to be expressed and clothed again in the costume of the day.

Sometimes being in the mould of the incarnation is taken to mean we should be silent witnesses, living among the people (use words if you must). But Jesus became a proclaimer and a teacher:

> From that time on Jesus began to preach, 'Repent, for the kingdom of heaven is near' . . . Jesus went throughout Galilee, teaching in their synagogues, preaching the good news of the kingdom, and healing every disease and sickness among the people. (Matthew 4:17, 23)

All four Gospels recall this activity of verbal communication as a rhythm of stirring truth that challenged the will and stirring truth that enlightened the heart. The identification principle took Jesus down the road of preaching and teaching.

He proclaimed and taught with authority, replacing a mode of teaching that always drew on what another learned rabbi had said about the Torah with a style that was vivid, direct, urgent and personal. Above all, it was clothed with an amazing authority that was recognizable both on earth and in the spirit realm. 'What is this? A new teaching – and with authority! He even gives orders to evil spirits and they obey him' (Mark 1:27).

The way Jesus communicated is vital for us to recover today. If we were to follow the ministry method of Jesus, there would be an immediate effect on our preaching and teaching. We would recover confidence in Scripture. Even many contemporary evangelicals (who have wanted to be Bible people) become uncertain about its authority and its use, and do so on the grounds that the incarnation of Jesus suggests our lives are more important than what we actually say. But this is to misread the implications of the identification of Jesus with us. Ask what the attitude of Jesus was to the Old Testament and only one answer is possible. The Word embraced Scripture as the word. The Word of God equals Scripture and vice versa. What God says, the Bible says, and vice versa (John 10:35). And he expressly said that the Spirit of truth would speak to them and call to mind all that Jesus taught (John 15:26). It was an exciting, specific period when the Bible was growing. If we claim to follow the Lord Jesus Christ, we cannot set aside his attitude to Scripture. We must follow him there too. For the Bible itself is of the pattern of the incarnate Word made flesh, truth mediated through the people who wrote it down. Their human personality was not set aside. Paul is a different writer from Matthew. It was a unique juxtaposition of word and flesh that created Scripture. Incarnation and Scripture are woven from the same cloth. It is not permissible to split the cloth.

When the Son of God was here, he was no truth whisperer. Unlike John the Baptist, Jesus was not a mere herald, for he was what he preached and he preached what he was. John was a voice crying in the wilderness. Jesus strode from the wilderness to proclaim in the power of the Spirit that the time of waiting was over and God's clock had struck. The time of reading about it in the paper, as it were, was over. The kingdom had come and God's message was now incarnated on the earth.

Jesus had no-one acting as Aaron to his Moses (Exodus 7:1), silently standing there while others proclaimed his identity and his demand. Jesus engaged in making direct, urgent appeals to the people, lifting up his voice so it would be clearly heard above the cacophony of background sounds that detract from hearing and responding. Reading the Gospels makes it impossible to avoid it. Jesus believed that direct proclamation was the God-ordained means of getting the truth into circulation: 'Let us go somewhere else – to the nearby villages – so that I can preach there also. That is why I have come' (Mark 1:38). Immediacy constrained him.

At heart it is a clear question of authority, and therein is the challenge for its contemporary application. Like lecturing only more so, the very activity of preaching is to talk *to* people rather than *with* them. It is monologue, not dialogue. The late modern attitude to truth comes out clearly in the reaction we have to words like 'preaching', 'lecturing' and 'monologue'. They are pejorative words, suspicious of biblical authority. Powerful preaching has to go back on the map in national life, not be seen to be the last gasp of an outfit profoundly out of touch with its age.

People in the twenty-first century tend to base their beliefs on experiences. But no distinction is made between experiences. And so we become confused if all our experiences are equally valid. We do need to tell what is good religion from what is bad. We've seen far too much of the downside, the cults, or those religious sales operations that depersonalize people. As a consequence, our age is so vulnerable to deception. Without the Book of God, the Bible, we should have no reliable knowledge of the spiritual realm. Belief must be based on something. A relationship with the ultimate power can only be based on what is shown to us.

Modernity wanted to grapple with the Bible through the lens of ordinary processes that go on in our world every day rather than have recourse to unproven external interventions. Yet the Bible is a supernatural book. Its writers speak with a single voice. 'What we have written are not our own words,' they say. 'The Spirit of the Creator took hold of us and moved us to write. Everything we have written has authority. All we have written is true.' Seized by prophetic fire that was not from their own kindling, those contributing to the body of evidence insisted that God had acted.

But is there not inspiration and inspiration? Maybe the biblical writers were inspired in a general way with ideas about the Creator and the world, as we are inspired by a sunset. Truth is what you find out for yourself, surely?

Yet every lawyer knows that in an important document, the words are important. The absence or presence of a few words alters the impression conveyed. Scripture is breathed out by the breath of the Creator: expired, not just inspired by those who wrote. The Creator is a speaking God, communicating with us in ways that we can talk about, not just experience. Through language in different types of genre, biblical witness is coherent and can be grasped. It is divine self-disclosure expressed in the tangible, physical life of scroll and book. The source of what we know of God is sacred text on which is imprinted the mind of God, embodied truth in keeping with the embodied life of the incarnate Lord who sought to be sought.

Journey's end

Christian conviction is incarnational because it has a quite definite focus. Rather than being a diffuse message on a range of philosophical ideas or social commentary, our conviction stems from total confidence that this world has been power-fully visited by God. God with us, becoming one with us: this is what was going on in the events that were secretly unfolding. And it was taking place after centuries of preparation and build-up. The identification of Jesus was rooted in a tradition, in a given culture shaped by divine input and by time.

This build-up and preparation is part of the answer to those who say that God must reveal himself more widely than in Jesus. One man, one place, one time seems too limiting when God makes himself known. Yet this emphasis on Jesus' uniqueness is the greatest strength of Christianity. The uniqueness of Jesus is a red line we cannot cross without gaining the religious world but losing our soul.

For communication to make any sense to anybody, it has to be coherent. A mixed message will confuse and bring different responses. An advert that appeared to be selling two different products would not work. A politician making a speech with points that contradicted each other would simply not get his or her message across (not that this usually bothers politicians). We know about rational communication in our everyday lives. If someone was to say, 'Have some fish. I like carpets. The moon is green,' we would be quick to respond that the lights are on but there was no one at home. And we would notice immediately if an email became garbled in transmission. Those who protest indignantly against God taking a human form only once haven't really thought about what a rational communication from God (or from anybody else) actually involves.

If God showed himself through this person or through different avatars, how would we build up a coherent picture of what God is like or what he wants from our lives? Jesus was not born in Manchester. He was born in ancient Israel, whose understanding and experience of God provided the right context for the good news.

If all the supposed manifestations of God were the same, the picture we would build up from the claims to be God on earth would be totally confusing. And there would be no definitive original of which we could say, 'This is what God is like.' The incarnations of an avatar are not the definitive manifestation of God on earth.

C. S. Lewis was right. If we could sum up the contrast between real Christianity and all rivals in one word, it would have to be 'grace', the self-giving of God, the self-sacrifice of God for a world that turned its back on him (and continues to do so). Every other message involves humanity reaching upwards or outwards (or even inwards) in search of God. The whole significance of Jesus is that God has reached out to us.

Opening a seismic crusade in New York city in 1957, Billy Graham had this to say:

> We have not come to put on a show or entertainment. We believe that there are many people here tonight who have hungry hearts. All your life you've been searching for peace, joy, happiness, forgiveness. I want to tell you . . . you can find everything you have been searching for in Christ.[1]

It is beyond the scope of this book to probe how Jesus Christ can be set forth as the journey's end, the fulfilment of the quest and answer in the search engine of human insecurity and sinfulness. Can we be saved by a Christ we do not know? These are pivotal issues in a pluralist world. There is historical synchronicity between the global expansion of the Christian church in the 'great century' and new-found awareness of major world faiths and belief systems its missionaries encountered. We may well say that we can learn from other religions. But the importance of revealed truth and the uniqueness of God's identification with our humanity through its fullest expression in Jesus cannot be surrendered without severe loss of compassionate and passionate authority.

We cannot soft-pedal the amazing claim about Jesus as a once-for-all embodiment of God. To do so is to abandon the truth that God makes himself known in a consistent and intelligible way that we can get hold of. It is in the life, death and resurrection of Jesus that the disturbed and disturbing world can find the answer to life. This gives the church a definite message to take out of its upper room. A confident church does not downplay the truth of the incarnation. It rejoices in it. There needs to be passion and gutsy communication of it, sensitive yet bold. Myriad voices fill the airwaves and crowd cyberspace. Why should the Christian church not make itself heard in the marketplace?

The ear and the eye

There is another reason why communicating Jesus must be incarnational. The message about him must be rooted in messengers. The message about an embodied God must be embodied within relationships between those who communicate and those who hear.

Language has always been separated into two components: content and style. The content relates to what we express – that is, the meaning or subject matter of statements. Style of language relates to how we express ourselves, rather than the content we express. Our challenge is that the seismic shift away from modernity towards a place as yet to be defined has resulted in altered ways of handling information. For reasons that are beyond the scope of this book, the ear is less privileged than it used to be. The ear is less in favour. The eyes have it.

Far more of us these days are visual learners. Auditory culture no longer holds our short attention span. We do not now follow an argument, even when it is carefully reasoned and logically structured. A TV and film culture is dominant. Advertisers ply their wares and have reshaped the world in their images. People need to *see* before they *hear*, or at least *see* at the same time. Image is powerful. Message begs to be embodied in something you can see and feel for its authenticity to be verified.

The message about an embodied God must be gift-wrapped within human messengers. To come alongside people and 'merely' proclaim will not accomplish the same results as when the message comes within a context; from someone who can be seen and heard, someone who can be communicated with, someone who comes alongside, someone who takes their side. Belonging comes first for many. Context is crucial. We have to experience a message that is embodied in something or someone. Non-church people no longer drop in. It takes a personal invitation from church folk to bring them over the threshold. Yet a culture of invitation is sadly missing in many of our churches.

The implications of this shift are decisive. As a community of faith, a welcoming church is imperfect but inevitable as a vehicle for communicating truth. Belonging and community are the medium for the message. Those who stress proclamation alone are full of wistful nostalgia, harking back to a previous era. Social action and practical service, especially if designed to reclaim the power of relationship, are vital to creating embodied contexts within which people can begin to see with open mind and heart.

Consider this. The essence of that cold 'R-word' – religion – is usually a blend of cosmology (the ultimate power behind the physical universe) and morality (how that power and presence shapes human life). Yet this picture of cosmology plus morality leaves out a mighty force in human experience. A focus on philosophy and ethics has little place for practice; for participation in the traditions of family, neighbourhood and broader currents of prevailing life. Belief is rarely a private affair. Doing things socially, with others, does not replace personal inspiration or individual awareness of the divine, but it does shape profoundly how these matters are experienced. True believers say things that those who have gone before will have said and sung. Faith and belonging go hand in hand. Faith is not like magic; it unites people together. Communities of the like-minded, like the church, are an essential society for the propagation of an incarnational faith. A network of relationships holds so many of our ultimate concerns as well as our everyday pursuits. Bold and rare are those who strike out on their own and stay that way.

Christian formation is about habits of the heart and life in combination with the like-minded. Joining with those who have similar values strengthens bonds when present or weakens bonds when absent. Faith transmission, or its lack, is at the heart of the slow death of Christian culture in our time. The impact of parents ceasing to communicate the faith to their children will result in a generation that scratched its head to think of a reason why they should believe. The idea that we should not teach or communicate faith to the next generation in the belief that they should be free to make their own choices is profoundly mistaken. It sounds right but it reflects a culpable failure of nerve. Competing pressures are immensely powerful but are no match for the power of close social bonds. Very few find their way to faith through instinct alone. An instinctual quest for God needs nurturing through teaching and belonging in order to find its expression in the life and times of the church of God.

Transmission of faith from one generation to the next rests upon faith being communicated and taught by parents to their children. To be sure, learning about God is insufficient unless backed up by living the good news. But why the incompatibilities? We were beguiled by the fallacy that it is better to wait until children are old enough to choose for themselves before inculcating what it means to be a Christian.

Ministry among the once and future church stands or falls on authenticity. Young people find a church to be far more compelling if it welcomes them royally and values them as individuals. A place to belong is the unchanged heart-cry; acceptance is a safe haven from the wild west of social media. Personal relationships are vital in an era when so much socializing is performed online: having those around them embody the close relationship with God as a life-orientation that they seek to evoke.

The power of narrative creates context. Much of biblical witness is expressed through story rather than propositions. In our time, story that enables people to see and paint a picture works better than logical structures of spoken words. Relevance and authenticity come because of identification with someone within it. Citizen voters respond to emotion for this reason; hearts are touched and open to do the task of inner visualization. Listening to reasons why a given course of action makes sense has less currency. Place-making, long neglected, is paramount today. Rooted beings come from somewhere. Rootless voices sound and resound in the wind but will not find lodging in the heart.

Eternal message – changing destination

The good news is a changeless message addressed to changing circumstances. Content remains the same. It is the address on the email that keeps changing.

An intelligent hermeneutic and application brings the timeless into the realm of the time bound. It is a constructive task fused with imagination as it engages in building bridges between worlds. Twenty-first-century folk find it harder and harder to believe that the Creator speaks to people in a clear-cut way. We have entered an age of pluralism where everyone has their own name for God. Those who appeal to biblical authority seem to have closed minds. The Bible is surely of its time. Old certainties will not do any more. Claims of an objective world not coloured by our experience became automatically suspect. We are all subjective now.

How much our age presents dynamic and bewildering flux! What are these strange times we inhabit? They are also contradictory. For instance, our economic system is based on some people doing better than others. Yet any message that seems to smack of entrenched inequality is automatically suspect. We live in egalitarian times.

'On what basis are you telling me what to do?' is an implicit litany that throws off shackles of any kind and cries havoc against moral restraint. Modern people far prefer to go their own way in life and whistle their own tunes. The attitude to the word and sacred text in an internet age has eroded any concept of authority. In the democratizing of thinking and views, everyone is his or her own interpreter. Yet we still want truth. We want to know what is right; we want a framework within which to live life, a sacred canopy of meaning and purpose. Modernity has slain its millions and left a black hole of emptiness.

Truly, the tectonic plates have shifted so as to remake continents of thought.

Social change has been dramatic: the breakdown of deference, respect for minorities, the equality of women, awareness that race, class and gender work together to produce deeply unequal outcomes – these have all become stock-in-trade attitudes of most in a liberal society that is rapidly post-Christian.

Shopping profoundly shapes the way we think and the way we live now. Around us, the spiritual supermarkets of our time beckon with shrill insistence. Aisles are crammed full of so-called necessities, inviting us to choose whatever we take into ourselves and consume. From gadgets to holidays, we can buy whatever will compliment us and bolster the inner story we recount. Social media has granted voice and choice to many – but also coarsened public debate with intimidation. The titans are the few new technocrats who run the world and manipulate the rest of us (or the advertisers whose currency is image-making). Never was so much owed by so many to so few.

Our times have seen the collapse of value; a spiritual stock-market crash. Pick-and-mix experiences, free-wheeling beliefs, an undermining of what is important when the only things you value are the things you can count – these have shaped a speed and noise culture that is both pervasive and invasive. Religion has been chased out of the public square, relegated to private indulgence.

Surely it is high time for a new wave of apologetics? Attuned to these social earthquakes, the church must once again sing its song and tell its story, chastened yet nurtured in confident faith. But what songs should we sing that will resonate with the fragile self that greets us on the morning train?

The Seven Songs

According to the writer Christopher Booker, there are seven basic plots to the endless stories people tell that encapsulate human experience. Here is a proposal. Labelled 'The Seven Songs', it probes whether the larger themes playing in ancient texts have resonance for contemporary people. It invokes texts from Ecclesiastes. Yet in a different take on apologetics for twenty-first-century people, it asks if there is a master song, a unified symphony of clear and cohesive beliefs that plays beyond what goes on inside the church to the wider world. Does Christianity make sense? Is it coherent? Do we stand under the canopy of plausibility? Do our contemporaries have a better, more coherent view of the world?

It is high time to end the retreat to the margins of society. What price great sermons to the faithful when most of the population are either taking their children to football training or frequenting supermarkets? Far too often, the church just hedges, but even proclaiming and serving with indefatigable enthusiasm and boundless conviction will not cut through to the heart if the whole thing looks implausible.

The hallmark of modernity was that people asked a basic question of something that had been claimed: 'Is it true?' More than before, in the new mindset in society that is emerging, the concern is 'Does it work for me?' Validity and authenticity are now joined in holy matrimony. To construct a plausibility shelter over the hope-filled message of God becoming one of us is an urgent task. A truly incarnational faith demands an effect in that same real and material world that Jesus embraced.

Other ways of living and being in the world are widely imagined and celebrated. Despite its own assumptions being rarely questioned, in the public mind it is widely assumed that science has driven a cowering church off the field. A technocratic, managerial sort of world has little room for Christian claims.

If communication be the topic, the task of going to where the people are is apologetics. Sitting where the people sit, as Ezekiel was called upon to do (Ezekiel 3), was, in the career of the Christ, complemented with relevant proclamation. Jesus spoke not as the scribes but with the gift of clothing his speech in the thought forms of his audience. Parables spring to mind because they sprang to his. His illustrations, his stories, illumined his message. His was no polished rhetoric but language that lived.

His great apostle, his chosen vessel, Paul was dispatched across the Mediterranean to plant the gospel flag everywhere the door would open. Paul was keenly aware of his audiences and knew how to clothe his message accordingly. Mars Hill in Athens was witness to an apologetic masterpiece; the greatest thinker of his day, he was a philosopher in the playground of the philosophers, both defending faith and proclaiming his gospel. Whether he won over his hearers is uncertain, but what cannot be disputed is that in his disputation Paul was being intensely incarnational, embodying a living message.

Who is doing this work today? There is great need of it. Credible people who can pass muster in the marketplace of ideas must rise to the challenge of our time and take it seriously so the church may be taken seriously. Either that or the hostility of thinking people to the message of Christ must be disarmed, their guns spiked. It is vital that the living message be living and embodied. Modern people ask much less, 'Is it true?' This is not uppermost now. Authenticity has become the test of truth. Christian roots that held society together have withered. Secular life and thought has captured and colonized everything. It has chased religion from the public square. Private faith is just about acceptable. An intellectual flowering is needed, combined with passionate imagination to lift the lid on what it means to be human and to flourish as a human being. Incarnational work requires us to go to where people are, to ask questions and find out what is going on in their lives, not just 'tell' the people.

There is prior work to be done. Big claims and ultimate issues are emphatically up for discussion. Does the contemporary church have faith that beliefs and doctrines in Scripture play to wider human concerns? It is a safe assumption that a growing number of people not in meaningful contact with a church (and those who are) suppose Christianity has little to say to what is going on in their lives. They have not heard the startling news, that the good news of Jesus resonates with the deepest needs of the human heart that sings in the night.

Addressing concerns matters. Even with politicians, the medium is the message. Those who espouse calm, dignity and conviction will cut through to the heart in confused times. Politicians increasingly know they have to respond to the concerns of voters rather than continue regardless with their agenda. The much-debated 'populism', for instance, speaks of a rage against the political establishment that ignored grievances. Only ostriches will fail to at least try to remedy the impact of global forces and industrial change, unsettling cultural values and the decline of community. Intelligent, enterprising global leaders will double down on underlying issues and discern opportunities behind our troubled times to reshape things. After all, this was how social and political reform always proceeded.

Dietrich Bonhoeffer, a classically trained musician, wrote of 'a kind of *cantus firmus* to which the other melodies of life provide the counterpoint . . . Where the ground bass is firm and clear, there is nothing to stop the counterpoint from being developed to the utmost of its limits.'[2] Though the song introduces twists in pitch and style, counterpoint and refrain, the *cantus firmus* is enduring melody playing somewhere within the composition. It provides firm support to avoid going out of tune.

The incarnational way of being the church in the world helps us combine the songs of humanity with the song of God. Listening to the underlying themes playing in our life and times can create considerable resonance with the biblical world view. In bringing the liberating message to our peers, we should take no prisoners. After all, what holds life together when everything is coming loose?

The first song – the song of wonder

> As you do not know the path of the wind,
>   or how the body is formed in a mother's womb,
> so you cannot understand the work of God,
>   the Maker of all things.
> (Ecclesiastes 11:5)

Can you respond to the wonder of a cosmos that stretches on and on into the night?

The starting point for the church has been God, Jesus or the Bible. They are not where people start from today. Contemporary concerns are strong, though. We worry about plastic in the oceans, ivory poaching or renewable energy. We worry about eating meat, or about global warming. Secular life labels it 'the environment': the church calls it 'the creation'. And this sense of creation, of this vast arena made on purpose, can restore a world drained of wonder by hungry commerce and technocratic life. A biblical world view resonates with ultimate concerns. The first song addresses the fantastic place where we live and sings to an aesthetically ordered world.

The second song – the song of the man in the mirror

> [I wanted to] see what was good for mortals to do under heaven
> during the few days of their life. I made great works; I built
> houses and planted vineyards for myself; I made myself gardens
> and parks. (Ecclesiastes 2:3–5, NRSV)

What is it about us that we are born with an unceasing quest for depth, creativity, communication and curiosity? Will someone tell us our secret identity? Science has little to say about the value we need in order to thrive. The church has capitulated to a bullying humanism that provides no basis for the value people have, the personal implications of human significance or the sanctity of life. What does it mean to be truly human? We are not on a conveyor belt like the one formerly used on game shows for the winners. Life is not about a range of experiences and things that pass in front of us from which we choose. An appeal to think hard about ultimate issues must focus on the collapse of value. Where will space for the human dimension be found in world futures where robots have taken over?

The third song – the song of the Creator

> He has made everything suitable for its time; moreover, he has put a sense of past and future into their minds, yet they cannot find out what God has done from the beginning to the end. (Ecclesiastes 3:11, NRSV)

Is there an ultimate power that corresponds to what's in here? The philosopher Kant has on his tombstone words that summarized his writings: 'Two things fill my mind with ever increasing wonder – the starry heavens above and the moral law within.' Is there a message that can bring together what is 'out there' and the secret knowledge we have of our own psychodramas? It is all very well to cower under the secular onslaught. But what do our hearers think is ultimate or the power that rules? Does it have anything to do with the value we need as a thirsty person craves water? God is the basis of all reality, a necessary being that cannot but exist, not just another thing in the universe of things, or a mental concept like concepts of anything else in the physical world.

The fourth song – the song of the hunter and the hunted

Again I looked and saw all the oppression that
    was taking place under the sun.
  I saw the tears of the oppressed –
  and they have no comforter;
    power was on the side of their oppressors –
and they have no comforter.
(Ecclesiastes 4:1)

Who has spoiled the beauty of the world? The modern programme had little place for the reality and depth of evil. Sin was deselected. The problem with people, it was said, is not some deep-dyed tendency towards evil but wrong actions by individuals and societies that were bad. Yet the evil and sin unleashed on the world caught most civilized people by surprise. Where on earth did that come from? In Germany, home of rationality and the Enlightenment, holocausts should hardly ever happen. Encouraged by politicians and theologians, the twentieth century became trapped in liberal optimism, hoisted upon its own petard. Yet our problems are that we are both hunter (engaging in destructive behaviour) *and* hunted (with harm done to us). We weave life as a rope with two strands. The political Left emphasizes the latter in terms of the impact of collective structures; the political Right stresses personal actions and feckless people. But Christian truth probes the intents of the heart, the motivation. Can contemporary people account for evil in their various world views?

The fifth song – the song of tragic reaping

God will call the past to account . . .
God will bring every deed into judgment,
  including every hidden thing,
  whether it is good or evil.
(Ecclesiastes 3:15; 12:14)

Ideas in theology are like the pendulum that swings from side to side. Twentieth-century people protested that it is inconsistent with the generosity of God's love to make the forgiveness of sins dependent on the death of Jesus. But there was a far deeper reason why it became fashionable to turn away from seeing the death of Jesus as an atoning sacrifice. We didn't think we needed saving. As we have seen, there is always the irresistible push towards payment in human affairs. Someone must pay. The moral law and conscience confirm that actions have consequences. Yet will the correct invoices be paid and justice prevail? Christianity does not believe in the law of karma. We do believe in the cross and its transforming power resulting in profound forgiveness. Yet how does a philosophy of life stand up in the face of suffering, the big challenge to theism or any perspective?

The sixth song – the song of a haunting future

They do not know what is to be, for who can tell them
how it will be? (Ecclesiastes 8:7, NRSV)

An appeal to those outside the church to think hard about ultimate issues must invite people to probe the issue of hope. When will the sigh be stilled? What is their view of the world that can accommodate hope? The big narratives of modernity such as progress have collapsed. In uncertain times, pessimism is routine. What are the ideals that are worth striving for? Writers who are concerned about the state of society should be able to make common cause with a church that yearns to build a better world under God. What about death and the great questions of our mortality?

The seventh song – the song of joyful freedom

> I have seen something else under the sun:
>   The race is not to the swift
>   or the battle to the strong,
>   nor does food come to the wise
>   or wealth to the brilliant
>   or favour to the learned.
> (Ecclesiastes 9:11)

Can we find a liberation that resolves our inner tensions surrounding the past, the present and the future? This is why the message of the cross is so utterly true to life. It is the message that must be proclaimed again in the twenty-first century. Every time we sin, we rubbish other people's value and break God's law. Fail to recognize that and you either trample on someone and say that they don't matter or, much worse, you minimize God's law and say that God doesn't matter. It comes down to the personhood most fully found within God and that Jesus identified with as a human incarnation. Jesus died to pay the price for our sins. The contemporary church is unsure how to present this and make our case. Yet transferring our wrongdoing to Jesus as the global sin-bearer offers a way out, the only exit from what we have done; divine forgiveness from the past, power for the present and hope for the future.

This way of probing world views that people have takes the battle to the hearts and minds of those we live among, especially those who have supposed that the good news of Jesus is not good news for them. It endeavours to go where the people are and engage with them on their terms and turf. Exposing the hollowness of contemporary assumptions is a route to showing that faith in Christ is not some antiquated belief we all thought was a museum piece, but a dynamic approach to life and eternity.

13

Transformative action and divine doorways

The cultural captivity of the Christian church

It was baffling: deeply disturbing. In Jesus' parable of the sheep and the goats, anguish is not recorded and can only be conjectured. How was it that they completely missed him?

It is a question the contemporary church wrestles with. Few local or national churches have not. 'What is Christian about Christian community engagement?' How do we remain faithful to Christ and Scripture in our mission? By what criteria should we evaluate church-related social action? Should we not just get on with winning a lost world and forget about trying to do something about the local community, let alone transforming society (a lost cause, surely – let the church be the church!). After all, humans are made for companionship with the divine. We believe we have insight into how humanity, fashioned in God's image, can flourish, and ought not to surrender that insight to social work. Yet we were made to talk on two legs. Evangelism and social action are integral to our witness. They fit together because, as we have been exploring, post-Christian people will not generally *hear* our message unless they can *see* it embedded in practical action and embodied within an authentic church that cares about its community.

But should we erode the distinction between internal and external dimensions of church? One church engages in direct evangelism. Preaching and teaching are its great emphases. Care is taken with sermons. Children's work is lively. The youth group is growing. Mothers and Toddlers regularly use one of the church rooms. Plans are unfolding to design ministry to various groups in society that will involve some combination of social care and invitation, of action and word. All sorts of activities go on for young people, or men, or those over 50. Questions of faith and the meaning of life will be discussed in an informal and friendly environment. The church runs a cafe that reaches out to the community.

A church down the road might try to serve in a different way. It is less gathered, less concerned about maintaining careful identity and walls of separation. Caring for those who are homeless or vulnerable will be part of its DNA. It is quite comfortable playing host to many local organizations who do good work but are not explicitly Christian. On an average day, you might see a range of community groups in the building. They come into the church. They are part of its footprint. They have become integral to its community and rub shoulders with it. It is not just about income. For the leaders, the big thing is being with the people, being among them. Conversion is talked about less here. It does not matter if it is not the church undertaking activity within its four walls; in fact it is a church without walls. All kinds of social purposes are permissible if ethical. Let others come and do it. Let others be contracted, mandated.

Is this Christian? Is it 'Christian' only when that is the label on the tin? Does it have to be Christian in word and deed, explicitly so, in order to qualify? Is doing what is done in a loving and welcoming manner or engendering a Christian spirit sufficient (and is that the same as 'the Spirit')? As we saw in the previous chapter, action done in the spirit of the incarnation takes place through relationships that enable others to see what is happening through someone who embodies the living Jesus.

Community engagement can seem to be a second-class carriage in the mission train, as if the most important freight is in the first-class carriage marked 'direct evangelism'. It can seem the slippery slope down to a more fuzzy perception that surely the Spirit of God is present wherever there is honesty, social justice and effective peacemaking. That perception was not perhaps so wide of the mark. How can they not be in some way signs of the kingdom to which we are moving if that kingdom has qualities such as these as its hallmark (under God of course)?

It helps focus our thinking on the immense value people have. Human lives matter. Personhood counts. We only have to ask, 'Who are the people that Jesus identifies with today?' to be in the challenging terrain of Matthew 25.

The cast of characters in Jesus' parable in Matthew 25 presents a curious line-up – the sheep, the goats, the King and the needy. But Jesus says that the cast of characters is actually less than the listeners might think. For the astonishing point being made is that the last two dramatis personae were the same. They missed the King for one obvious reason. They failed to recognize him.

Jesus did not only model incarnational service: through his healings he taught it. Matthew 25 is the clearest example. Evangelicals skirt around it and leave it to liberal Christians or purveyors of the social gospel. But it breathes the very spirit of the incarnation: 'whatever you did not do for one of the least of these, you did not do for me' (Matthew 25:45).

The vision was hindered by lack of recognition. They just didn't see him. How was it possible to miss their King when he turned up? It was baffling. It was profoundly disturbing. The King had come. The puzzled questioning had begun with a curtain-raiser – another 'when' moment that delineates time: 'When the Son of Man comes in his glory' (Matthew 25:31), there will be Separation Day. In that time of distinguishing, sheep and goats will no longer be in the mixed flocks common in the Middle East. Their separation will be on the basis of their service record, the outworking of an authentic faith.

Whether they recognized the one they were dealing with is not really the point. The outworking of their faith in feeding, clothing and visiting the vulnerable was a strong signpost to whether it was genuine. Faith without works, as James says, is dead. It is not the faith that gives us position, standing and status with God (James 2). It is, however, a clear guide to its authenticity. How do we know that faith is for real, or are we kidding ourselves by mouthing the right words? Does feeding in the right flock (as goats did with the sheep) show what sort we are? Practice and cultural habit are no more sufficient than words by themselves. The fruit must be in our conduct and in the powerful but unwitting combination of compassion and strength we bring to service for the King. Yet there is another powerful truth here knocking to be let out.

The King is emphatic. He is one with those in need.

> I was hungry and you gave me something to eat, I was thirsty and you gave me something to drink, I was a stranger and you invited me in, I needed clothes and you clothed me, I was sick and you looked after me, I was in prison and you came to visit me.
> (Matthew 25:35–36)

It is not just that these are the kind of people he associates with. The weak and vulnerable, 'the least of these', are dignified by his standing with them and for them. It is a summons to action, but it is also a story about the identification of Jesus with our humanity. 'I' was a stranger. This is not the King in disguise. Yet what enables the King to say 'It was *me*'?

It goes back to the question as to who are the sheep. Let all those who celebrate the thought of the Son of Man seated on 'his throne in heavenly glory' (Matthew 25:31) follow the intriguing direction of travel in the parable. The judgment is universal. It is all the nations that are gathered. Then comes the determination. All are summoned. Those who are meek and have submitted themselves to the King (symbolized by the sheep) have carried out their day-to-day lives through serving. Whatever was not done for the followers of Christ was not done for him. But the deeper truth is not that it was done 'with me in mind' – it was *me*. The complete identification of Jesus stands out. But with whom?

On the face of it, this parable is teaching that we must learn to look for the face of Christ in the homeless, in the sick, the imprisoned and the poor. Down the years, Christians have used this parable to communicate the need for caring of all kinds: prison ministry, the sick and the homeless. The implications turn around one simple question: 'Who are "the least of these"?' The question is similar to that raised by the good Samaritan – 'Who is my neighbour?' And we know the answer to that one.

Jesus is saying in effect, 'If I stood in front of you sick, unclothed and in prison, you would care for me! Do it for those in need for my sake.' It is not so much seeing the face of Christ in the poor and needy as identification. We could take the view that acts of caring should be done to believers, to the sheep who have submitted themselves to Christ the

King. The King is not within them in disguise, but he is very much on their side. Jesus is here declaring his solidarity with the sick, homeless and imprisoned. The care of people in Jesus' name is done *for* him. In sympathetic association, it is also done *to* him.

What enables the King to say 'I' was in prison?

The King is standing shoulder to shoulder, as it were, with common humanity. The church has had a disgraceful record when it comes to treatment of people who are not in our fold, people like us. There are, to be sure, a hundred flowers blossoming every minute of every day, responding to human need through acts of service. But we cannot thereby dismiss the enormously intriguing challenge posed by this parable. Matthew 25 summons us to undertake loving service for the vulnerable. Followers of Jesus are called to give value to weak and vulnerable people – to treat them as the brothers and sisters of the King. If we started modelling the insight that people are important, those who think the Christian church is against human dignity might think again. If we truly believe in the immense value of humankind, we would aim for social transformation and not just acts of caring. The imperative today is recognition that we are not really dealing with the problem of the present day or the reality of people's lives.

Let's get on with feeding the hungry and clothing the destitute; let's get on with prison ministry, but let's not question the system that shunts people into conditions such as these. Let's only talk about the involvement of the church in addressing social relationships in some very precise ways. Why does the social conservatism many Christians espouse lead to not questioning the system? Why just shine a light in the darkness and not choose to confront it?

What, after all, are the conditions that create the prisoners, the hungry, or the poor devoid of the necessities of life? Those passionate to change our world can be heartened by the parable, as well as those who are committed to loving service. Those working for the transformation of the conditions that produce such hardship – the power structures that disfigure humankind such as racism – can be glad that it is the King on the throne who stands in solidarity with the oppressed. His power will trump the rulers of this world who throw their weight around for a while and enjoy their cruelty.

Looking back at some of the great social struggles of the past, it is hard to avoid the conclusion that the church has been on the wrong side. It has not taken the side of the weak and vulnerable but the side of the powerful, seeing the cry for justice as subversive activity. The church has simply not had the vocabulary to address the crimes of racism or gender-based violence. Surely we failed to realize how much we were captive to our culture and therefore unable to speak into it. Yet what concerns us now is the future. What response will we make for those who need bread tomorrow? What will we say to those whose hearts break through relational pain and distress? Why should we put up any longer with the fettered lives of our contemporaries? What are the great causes we want to get behind?

This does not go down well with those who want to restrict faith to the private sphere, who will applaud acts of loving service but will cease their applause when Christians attempt to address the social injustice that produces the conditions requiring such ministry. This is morally suspect but also deeply illogical. It is to say that acts of charitable service towards slaves were acceptable but the whole system of subjugation and brutality that produced it should not be challenged. It is to say that helping victims of domestic violence is praiseworthy but the system that generates it must not be questioned. The one is legitimate Christian concern; the other out of bounds.

It is to say that we should help the poor who are trapped in poverty but not do anything about the attitudes and scapegoating that keep them there. It is to say that weightier matters of justice and mercy and faith should be neglected while the emphasis is placed on smaller things. Jesus called such partisans 'blind guides': camel swallowers (for they dismissed the issues God cared most about). As his younger brother remarked, faith without action is dead (James 2:17)!

That has been questioned ever since movements to abolish slavery set a new tone in the world and Christian history. John Wesley, a fierce opponent of slavery, had this to say: 'Christianity is essentially a social religion; to turn it into a solitary religion is indeed to destroy it.'[1] His associates and successors knew no social distinction as they laboured with indefatigable fervour among all – rich and poor, educated or uneducated, masters and slaves, it mattered not. In theory at least, the democratic ideal emphasized the belief that all are equal in the sight of God. Since when has power and its consequences been off the agenda? Rulers and principalities that sustain the dark powers that haunt humankind feed off oppressive, mocking power. Their time will be up soon.

Uniquely placed – the existential crisis of our times

What it means to be incarnational is exercising most churches these days wherever they engage in loving service, on their doorstep or further afield. They know they need to be relevant to their communities and scratch where it itches, while being faithful to biblical calling. Yet with some noticeable exceptions, the church is not very good at connecting with contemporary society in a way that communicates our message such that people grasp that it is good news – and why.

The church will and should continue to place emphasis on fruit: 'Those who abide in me and I in them bear much fruit' (John 15:5, NRSV). Being fruitful entails so much that is both substantial and numerical. It has to be the outflow of a sense of holy presence and abiding, or dwelling deeply in Christ. Faithful pastoral work offers continuing opportunities to serve and engage in people's lives. The church is called to live out the values of God's kingdom. This includes such vital attitudes and practices as worship, sacrificial giving, generosity of heart and hand, flexibility and joyful service.

The challenge is that we can be myopic. We associate fruit with conversions, or disciples, to use the more contemporary word (even though the term hardly exists outside the Gospels and was probably restricted to the followers of Jesus in the days of his flesh – Acts 9:36 excepted). Paul's writings place emphasis on *believers* being transformed. There is a message there. Calls to prayer and solid intercession may well be the only force that will turn the tide. They used to call it revival. Only God can convert the nation. Yet being a people who carry the fire of hope must, has to, carry a lot of weight amid the pessimism and insecurity of social life today. There are numerous pathways by which the contemporary church is growing, notwithstanding the picture of managing decline that the church statistics sadly present.

Community engagement is one of those routes – bringing the church into contact with people it would never otherwise meet. What we do with opportunities is another matter. We walk on two legs. Holistic witness of proclamation and loving service was seen in what Jesus did. He proclaimed constantly, yet performed seemingly random healing miracles that showed his nature and identity.

As long as the essential message of the good news is neither obscured nor compromised, we must use every approach we can. Community mission is to scratch where society is itching, and itching strongly at the present time. Theologically, we have to sort out whether this is a biblical priority. Does the call to 'love your neighbour' lead us to spearhead social renewal? Should church be part of society or distant from it? How do we reconnect church to community and engage in bridge-building so that we bridge the gap to a changing world with the unchanging message of Jesus who identified with us deeply yet speaks to us?

Our societies are divided, fragmented and individualized. Communal bonds are weakening as people get on with their own lives. Where and how shall we bring people back together to heal our land?

Excursion – By way of example, incarnation and innovation: building a model of a strengths-based initiative

The church is St Winfrid's in Totton, on the edge of Southampton, named after the eighth-century apostle to Germany, Boniface. It is a cavernous building with spectacular arches (which gave their name to the project!). Only 80 years old, it was in need of serious attention. It is part of the Diocese of Winchester, which has been very supportive.

A church transformation has been under way here by a group of Christians who sought to nurture their faith in prayer and Scripture but who resolutely refused to be a club that exists for themselves. A relatively small congregation was obliged to take on its relatively large building and give it a positive future. As we sought to turn this large space inside out, into a community hub with a biblical church at its heart, it had to wrestle with questions that are resolutely theological. The church has sought not only to do works of caring and ministry to the needy but to work in a different way appropriate to our times. The world has moved on and paternalism does not work any more. The model of state welfare based on addressing the needs of the vulnerable is unsustainable.

The congregation sought to grow church in approaches to evangelism both new and old. Its latest manifestation is cafe church in the centre of town, an informal setting within which to explore faith. Alongside that it has walked the way of engaging with the locality, so its mission is holistic and well placed within its local setting. It started on that journey back in the summer of 2014 when it became clear that the church building needed serious attention. Rather than focus on the needs of the building, the church took a different path. What were the needs of the community that it could address? Could it reimagine church? What did it mean to be the people of God in Totton?

It is vital for churches who find themselves in that situation, and indeed for any community of faith, that it should be highly attuned to **purpose**. Purpose is the great 'Why?' question. It nurtures faith and positive confidence in God. It easily trumps the secondary, though inevitable, questions of 'How?' and 'What?' that churches are prone to get bogged down in. Fixation on divine purpose, combined with flexibility, will resolve many difficulties that stand in our way.

In the situation this church found itself in, we sought to ascertain what significant purpose would fit with the social mission that would accompany direct proclamation and witness. We found it in the growing and pressing problem of loneliness in society. For many, social responsibility ends at our front door. More than ever, each person is an island, cast adrift from spiritual and social moorings and the ties of community. Caring for others and those around is falling into disrepair. 'Where do I belong?' is the cry of the heart. 'Love thy neighbour' has never been a more pressing task.

Loneliness matters. Loneliness is the leprosy of our times. Few will admit to it. With lepers, people could see their plight, but it is far less obvious to communities when people are lonely. Loneliness has a harmful impact on human beings who were never made to be alone. Individualism is a blight on society. The church should feel this, for it touches the heart. In the UK, nearly one in five say they feel lonely often or always. One in ten say they have no close friends. Nearly half of over 75-year-olds say that the TV or pets are a main form of company. It is not just a problem for the elderly. More than a third of 18–34-year-olds worry about it, though many would be ashamed to admit it. Men aged over 35 are surprisingly vulnerable it seems.[2] Those surrounded by people might still feel alone and afraid. We can label this 'social disconnection', but it goes beyond labels. Inside we feel and fear. We are hardwired to seek connection with others. When we are lonely, we curl in on ourselves even more. Isolation is bad for your health and well-being. It has a negative impact on communities. Loneliness is the cry of the human heart.

The church believes in the primacy of relationship. We understand fully that the human heart can only find resolution by relating to God very differently. Yet we care about the cost of disconnection. We see people as people, not as resource or provision. We believe in their value. Those who come to look at whether they wish to join our community may be lonely and seeking companionship. The church has always been in the business of befriending the lonely, visiting the sick or housebound so that they have someone to talk to and do not feel so alone. Reconnecting through building relationships is vital. The church has a presence in every community. It can be social glue. We welcome people of all ages and social backgrounds. It is not just that churches are uniquely well placed to undertake activities that reduce isolation. Addressing isolation in society is our territory.

The particular direction in which the church was led lay in deploying the strengths of the building we had and the resource that was in front of us. But it was strengths-based in another way. The usual model of Christian social action has been dominated by the need to meet need. But instead of trying to tackle negative deficits in society as gaps where we should work, what if we sought to cultivate the positive, the strengths that people have latently? Could it be made to work if we were to address loneliness not by offering tea but by cultivating creativity and building relationships? The focus would be different. It would be about helping people discover gifts and talents they didn't know they had. It would minister to their sense of God-given worth.

Isolation is on many people's radar right now, both within churches and more widely. What St Wins explored was a twofold emphasis that is different from usual approaches. One was to be *intergenerational*, to combine early-years work on site with older people coming to us for various activities. There is growing interest in this approach as it is good for all concerned. We undertook a large-scale social research and community audit on the streets of Totton, which clearly highlighted this as being vital.

Harnessing the collective intelligence of those committed to the project saw a remarkable, creative journey unfold. Discerning the path meant a serious effort to understand our community, to immerse ourselves in its life and times, while never ceasing to look to God. For us, picking some low-hanging fruit meant taking hold very early on in the journey of a government grant to repair the roof of places of worship. It was a great encouragement to us that we were on the right path. 'Whatever your hand finds to do, do it with your might; for there is no work or device or knowledge or wisdom in the grave where you are going.'[3]

Yet the church also wanted to explore new directions in mission. Rapidly changing social conditions call for an incarnational church to adapt accordingly and consider developing such paths as social enterprise (not just the mission model of service founded long before charities existed). The church was at the forefront of a community timebank, so as to encourage renewal of social bonds and a chain reaction of generous giving in the community. A timebank is a national initiative like 'pay it forward', which sets up reciprocal acts of practical service in the community by local people who then 'bank' the hour and swap the time for something that someone else could do for them.

This is challenging. Many talk these days about how far we should be entrepreneurial. Though clearly not a Bible word, the church should be fearless in being on the lookout for opportunities. That's how the Salvation Army made such strides with its prayer-based combination of witness and action. We spoke with community doctors, leaders of civic authorities, Age Concern and similar groups – Church Urban Fund, Royal Society of Arts, universities, social entrepreneurs – anyone who could help us bring our vision to fruition. We needed to be experimental, not bringing our preformed ideas but allowing new shapes to emerge (Isaiah 43:19: 'I am doing a new thing').

The church did the groundwork in being a credible partner for statutory bodies and health authorities who were interested in social prescribing as a way of rerouting the anxious and the lonely to discover meaningful activity. As health care becomes unsustainable in society, keeping people active by intervening upstream will be vital – especially if it can be combined with openness to God. When the church made clear that it was open for business, as it were, some community groups became partners and welcome guests. This created opportunity that begged to be grasped with both hands. It was not crucial that we needed to own and do everything ourselves. Could the church keep its identity and not lose control while creating an environment within which others who sought to serve the common good could also work and flourish? Is this authentic Christian endeavour? 'Seek the peace and prosperity of the city ... Pray to the LORD for it, because if it prospers, you too will prosper' (Jeremiah 29:7).

The idea of 'the common good' is open to debate and critique. You could say that Jesus wrought miracles because they were signs of God's kingdom. Yet they were also undertaken out of compassion because Jesus, as one of us, sought the welfare and well-being of human beings. We simply have no way of knowing how many found their way to becoming his followers as a result.

For us, it was tough-going. Obstacles were like big boulders strewn across our path. The task is a continuing one. We came to a fork in the road. Developing this model even thus far required considerable outlay of labour, blood, sweat and tears, but also theological spadework in endeavouring to be clear about what we were doing and why. But above all it took prayer. It is better to try than not to attempt great things for God. A Christian eco-system with a vibrant church at its heart aiming to reach out to a world of lost and lonely people of different ages? It could not be more relevant to society. Could this be an effective strategy for mission?

Often we have to walk God's zig-zag paths rather than go straight to where we need to be. Being prepared to alter course is part of flexible faith because our trust is in the unchangeable Lord of the church. We walk one step at a time by the light we have. A future church plant is set to increase congregational strength by taking the work of the church further while building works go on. Because a cold building could not be secured without considerable investment, the existing congregation was compelled to relocate for a while. We had the choice of giving in and admitting defeat or embracing this positively and creating opportunity.

So we took the unusual decision to transfer to our local AFC sports ground. It is innovative and helps move the church from maintenance to mission. This is right where people are and where they come on a daily basis, especially 'hard-to-reach' men in our society not interested in church. In its journey through time, a frontier-crossing church going to where the people are: what could be more incarnational, transformational? A church that dared to change, not just its address but itself: watch this space . . .

Divine doorways – ten commandments for theological rationale

Because of the incarnation, the rationale for biblical social action is that we are responding to circumstances in which people find themselves, except that we are doing that on the basis of shared humanity and the Word made flesh. People need to *see* the love of God or they will not *hear*.

Just as Jesus was a frontier-crossing missionary and became embedded within a given culture, the identification principle compels us to wear the garb of our communities and allow for easy recognition. Yet more than anyone who has lived, before or since, Jesus was not swallowed up by his cultural setting. People could go through and beyond his culture; they could touch the divine.

A faith based on Matthew 25 is profoundly incarnational. The incarnation provides the ground for loving concern that enables people to do well and be open to God. What is meant by that? Is social action purely a means by which people become converted and part of the church?

To be biblical, Christian engagement with society (and the actions that follow) needs to have the dimension of openness to God, of what we will call 'divine doorways'. God is surely present, bidden or not, when there is positive relationship and authentic community. Pre-eminently, the church is about relationship, welcoming with open arms and an open heart both God and other people.

The test of what makes such activities as lunch clubs and coffee mornings (in which the church seems to specialize) specifically Christian is that of the divine doorway. Can people walk through to find God? Does God come through to find the listless, those baffled by their lives?

To be a divine doorway, here are ten commandments proposed as guidelines for social action.

1. Is it God-honouring (linked, as we have seen, to honouring humanity)?
2. Is an activity biblical in the sense of being consistent with Scripture?
3. Are there entrance moments – an openness to God as expressed in a Christian element somewhere within it that points beyond itself (an act of worship, a welcome to the Christian story, a welcoming invitation to church)? Does it have the quality of 'leaning towards Christ', to cite the fourth-century Gregory of Nazianzus: an open door for people to reach out to Jesus?
4. Does the activity reflect the love of Christ, both in its internal culture of restorative love and boundaries and showing the love of Christ to others?
5. Is the activity rooted in relationship extended by Christians who are genuinely interested in people? Does it promote relationship and joy?

6. Could it generate divine–human encounters and be a womb for new life? (Some theology saw human sexuality as needing the potential to create life.)

7. Is there awareness of sin and grace, to be vehicles for the grace of God? The potential for things to go wrong and for power to be destructive needs to be recognized. Remarkably few activities are morally neutral.

8. Will it further the mission of the church in that particular locality such that it is something the church could pray for without blushing?

9. Does it enhance the position of the church in being well placed to spread good news? Are there plenty of opportunities to evangelize?

10. Does it serve common humanity in that the aims of the church cohere with the aspirations of the community towards the common good of all?

Respecting the image of God in everyone is a creation ordinance. It is magnified considerably by the reality that the divine Word took human flesh. Human lives matter because that was the way God chose to reveal himself in the identification principle. Yet the worth that people have is not embodied within an isolated individual human being. It is shared, reciprocal and interwoven, distributed among those who call out the value of others. Who else out there is creating community today? Immense social forces are prising people apart. Faith creates authentic community. Jesus created community from a rag-tag collection of the disparate. When it has been true to itself and its Lord, the church has created community from racial and gender differences.

The Matthew menagerie of woes involved being in prison, destitute, hungry and vulnerable. Ultimately these are failures of relationship; they are human connections that have gone terribly wrong or fallen short. Is it enough to ground social action in human connections? There is an extra quality that is added to the mix when the church engages in social action. It is the dimension of being open to God, of divine doorways. This is the identification principle: the pattern of the walking, living channel to God through which the river of word and love poured for three years and has never ceased since.

These are questions that will continue to exercise the Christian church. We don't have to jettison the only truth that can save humanity to see that the church has usually been on the wrong side. Maybe if we really are a prophetic people (as opposed to saying that we are), we will not just see this retrospectively but at the time, or even in advance!

Incarnational service connects with the twenty-first-century crowd. The generation of famine relief and shoebox appeals is conditioned to look for works of caring as a hallmark of authentic Christianity. Upholding the value of personhood is a sacred, God-given task. The identification principle demands it. Taken together with the preceding chapters about passionate intercession, powerful proclamation and relevant apologetic, this chapter helps focus our thinking about the church's calling in the world. We affirm the importance of the biblical priority and centrality of evangelism and proclamation of Christ, but at the same time acknowledge the importance of the church's social witness. These friends walk together.

*'We will nourish our identity as a Christian foundation,
where God revealed in the person of Jesus Christ is
confidently and intelligently proclaimed. We will
commend an understanding of the human person
as a moral, spiritual and physical unity,
in which each dimension is equally important.'*
Winchester College, 'Moral and spiritual formation'

*'For just as the body is one and has many members,
and all the members of the body, though many,
are one body, so it is with Christ.'*
1 Corinthians 12:12, NRSV

14

The body of Christ and
the new humanity

Is there no continuity between the body of Christ and the body of Christ?

We have not yet come to the end of the story of the identification of the Son of God with our humanity.

The movement of identification led God down and down into the descent of incarnation. Jesus lived for a while on our level as one of us, sharing our life and pain. But the world rejected him, as if the Creator were a virus in the system rather than a deeply embedded part of the creation who gives everything meaning. But he was still going down; the pathway of descent leading down into the mire; he went where the deepest human need and failure lurk. They lifted him up for six hours, little glimpsing that the sentence meted out to him was payment for the sins of the world and a death for others. Then he went down, still descending, into the grave that closed its door on its most famous captive.

Then the pathway of identification led up, up, bursting through the grave, stone, seal and guard, pausing a little before ascending. Still higher, higher, drawing our humanity with him and taking our captivity captive until Jesus had reached the highest point of all. 'He who descended is the very one who ascended higher than all the heavens, in order to fill the whole universe' (Ephesians 4:10).

But though the Son had come home in triumph and with the guarantee of final victory, it was not so as to rest in that triumph and await the outcome of the victory. His identification with humanity had not been a passing interest, to be followed by an interesting project on the other side of the universe. Joining humanity had been for a purpose, so that through coming to where we were, the church would come to where he was and is and will be for ever.

Is the church an extension of the incarnation? There has only been one incarnation, the significance of which is profound. Yet the incarnation is extended into the new community, the body of Christ (signifying a new form of embodiment).

Destined to be dependent

How the theme of 'the body of Christ' emerged in the early church has been much discussed across the years. Every member is a conduit of divine love: that is the theme of Paul's much-quoted 'body-life' section in 1 Corinthians 12.[1] The giving of their gift depends neither on status nor deficiency of body and mind. It is rather dependency and mutuality that define our inclusiveness. This has rich significance for social attitudes towards those with disability, who challenge societies like ours addicted to performance and perfection of body shape. 'People who are the weakest and least presentable are indispensable to the body.'[2]

The theme of the body of Christ describes the interpersonal dynamics of the church, understood as a corporate and social entity. Paul did not introduce the organic image of 'the body' to address problems of human community. His use of the metaphor here is pregnant with significance. The Corinthian Christians had imbibed the idea of the church arranged according to status of knowledge and wisdom. Paul will have no truck with such a managerial disposition of the church. He has already interposed the cross as the leveller. Now he develops a rival account of the church as a human body. Bodily life, as Paul shows in 1 Corinthians chapters 6, 8 and 11, is a medium in which members are present to each other and integrally linked. The Christians in Corinth ought not to visit a brothel, they should be careful about offending fellow Christians over meat offered to idols, and they shouldn't misuse the body and blood of Christ.

Modernity is preoccupied with developing ever more efficient means, procedures, instruments or techniques to order the world. What is rarely on offer is the 'Why?' question, which is always fundamental. What are the purposes that the reduction of society and culture to sets of techniques would serve? Everywhere we look, whether in business, public services, technology, government or education, we see the unquestioned reign of performance. Production, consumption and technological control over nature are the order of the day to ensure tomorrow. The idea that organizes the Christian church is a very different one from the economic, technical rationality that rules the world. The church is rooted in the principle of representation, which is grounded in the concept of a 'person'; it is the body of Christ.[3]

The 'body of Christ' as a definite entity in space and time was shown in the one who trod the dusty roads of Palestine. As the physicality of a book expresses its message (even in an age of the ebook, most prefer this medium), 'that which . . . we have seen with our eyes, which we have looked at and our hands have touched' (1 John 1:1) was bodily representation of the divine. 'In Christ, all the fullness of the Deity lives in bodily form' (Colossians 2:9). Yet Paul also declares that 'He is the head of the body, the church' (Colossians 1:18). There has to be clear continuity here, albeit the Spirit of Christ inhabits a great crowd of witnesses which none but God can number. It is the identification principle.

Does the future have a church?

Does the church have a future is one question that exercises Christians. There is another, more important, question. Does the future have a church?

The church clearly featured in the past. God's people are caught up in the rhapsody of the love of God that extends through time and space. Traditions and previous life cannot just be ignored on any issue (unless manifestly unbiblical). We are not the first generation of Christians. Working out what it means to be God's people has been the unceasing wrestling in every age. Contextual, local versions of the body of Christ have been the way of things ever since African expressions of Christianity began to look different from Greek or Latin versions in the second century of our Lord.

God's people reflect God's continuous identification with humanity and are the advance guard of history, on the move with God towards final victory. We have profound insights about what it means to be a person and the people of God. Those with a secular philosophy contend that a paradigm devoid of faith and the Spirit is the best way of organizing life today. The Christian church dissents from this mindset profoundly. Without a spiritual dimension we are impoverished. Our secular age persists in redirecting human concerns away from God to people. Dignity is supposed to be advanced by jettisoning the right relation to God that is integral to our highest flourishing. In a powerful alternative vision, what it means to have a proper relation to God was lived out in the life and person of Jesus Christ. Look again at the incarnation and see how Jesus embraced thirty unremarkable years. In those Nazareth days, Jesus was a son, a brother, a neighbour, a friend. He displayed attention to others, watching life in the raw round. Yet he was surely attentive, supportive of the village.

We are a frontier-crossing crowd who are here to serve as Jesus did. Eschewing powerful forces that reduce humans to commodities, we are shaped by the conviction that every life has immense value, made in the mirror of the divine. What it means to be human is deeply rooted in the sacredness that people have and in the sense of community that both embeds and recognizes that (but only when internal cultures of churches and Christian organizations are consistently aligned). We have in our very hands rich biblical insights that mean we capitulate no more to the Constantinian capture of the church and consequent collusion with the violence that continues to disfigure our Christian witness.

The post-millennial generation can see plenty that's wrong with the world. Can it be right there's any amount of jobs that need doing to cleanse and restore the environment and care for the hurting while millions out of work are paid to do nothing? Yet to go from there to some dark secret at the heart of the human race is quite a step. Yes, they're tired of worn utopian dreams. But surely those are social evils. It doesn't mean there's something wrong with us. But God's Word calls us to look below the surface of things. There are obvious ways evil leaves its calling card. They are fruit. But what is the root? The root is the sin of defiance in the human heart, the lust, greed, hatred and envy that reproduce themselves in cultures and practices dishonouring God and devaluing those made in his image.

This is why the good news about Jesus is so powerful. We proclaim the empathy of God, the way that the Creator did not stay above the fray but entered it in full involvement with our messy humanity. We proclaim that he understands, and can therefore bring that insider knowledge of the human condition to bear upon the distress and suffering of the broken. But, armed with a full understanding of the atoning death of Jesus, we can go further. We can affirm that Jesus stood in solidarity not only with the victim of sin but with the sinning person. Because Jesus became the Lamb of God and took on himself the sin of the world, there is a way out. There is a place we can go to where the complicated patterns of our past are cut through by the power of forgiveness; a place of transfer where the normal way of living in the world becomes relegated to being an old humanity.

Romans 8 portrays the plan and purpose of God, moving inexorably towards this culmination. A vast scene of creation unfolds, a war-torn landscape characterized by blood, struggle, tears and pain, futility and death. Paul takes a daring historical panorama and says that these are the birth pangs. A new age is coming in which the children of God are the advance guard. The church holds the promise of victory and of deliverance from the old time of pain and death. It is working out its inner life and the lure of the future while being part of things. The church is not living six feet above contradiction and carrying on a charmed life above the fray. It is embedded and carries the struggle within itself:

We know that the whole creation has been groaning as in the pains of childbirth right up to the present time. Not only so, but we ourselves, who have the firstfruits of the Spirit, groan inwardly

as we wait eagerly for our adoption as sons, the redemption
of our bodies. (Romans 8:22–23)

The Spirit in us is very much part of that struggle too, involved,
committed to changing us to fulfil God's plan. Following the
pathway of identification with humanity trodden by the Son
of God, the Spirit of God becomes an integral part of the
process, an insider. The Spirit is not waiting for us to arrive
with an expectation at the point of destination. The Spirit
helps us en route, while we are still on the journey.

We are not immune from fearsome wrestling. Baffled at
times by the contrast between the pointed certainties we claim
and the rawness of things, the good news is that we are not on
our own. We have looked to the cross, which closes the door
on the old humanity while opening a door to the new. The
death and resurrection of Jesus brought us release from the
past and a new life, his life. And we have the Spirit who
communicates that new life to us and transforms us for the
future:

> The Spirit helps us in our weakness. We do not know what we
> ought to pray for, but the Spirit himself intercedes for us with
> groans that words cannot express . . . the Spirit intercedes for
> the saints in accordance with God's will. (Romans 8:26–27)

Romans 8 portrays, on a vast canvas, God's identification with
the human race. Having trudged through the mud and mire
of this world, the Son is now at the Father's right hand,
interceding (8:34). He intercedes for us as God but also as the
human he became. Within us is the Holy Spirit, linking up to
the man at God's right hand, joining the circuit of intercession
so that power can flow to help our weakness while we are part
of the battle. Jesus is the Moses on the hillside, holding up his

hands in intercession; the Holy Spirit is Joshua on the ground fighting with the troops (Exodus 17).

A groaning creation, a waiting emancipation, unaware that a group within it have already heard the good news of freedom – this is the struggle that Paul so vividly portrays here. His vision contains the Christian response to the perennial problem of suffering and points us to final victory and the consummation of God's identification with the human race.

Sin is the Bible word for acts and attitudes of defiance, and it has disfigured the world. The astounding landscape of creation has had buckets of paint thrown over it. We live in a world where humans do terrible things to each other, and no-one takes responsibility. At the beginning of Romans, Paul writes about the terrifying way that humanity threw off the chains of allegiance to the Creator. The day we began proudly to walk our own path to freedom and autonomy we were on a collision course with God. Paul writes that the consequence of this misguided and doomed act (confirmed every day) is that God leaves us to it: 'God gave them over' (Romans 1:24); 'God gave them over' (1:26); 'since they did not think it worth while to retain the knowledge of God, he gave them over to a depraved mind, to do what ought not to be done' (1:28).

Jesus was profoundly moved by the suffering he encountered. Indignant in the face of injustice and needless pain, again and again Jesus stretched out his hand to heal. It was a sign of the present and what was happening in their midst. But it was also a sign of the future. In Jesus, powers of the future were breaking through; the age to come seeping into the present. The healing miracles of Jesus were a signpost to the new age of God's kingdom, the true new age when there will be no pain and every tear will have been wiped from

every eye, when anguish will have been consigned to ancient
history.

> See, the home of God is among mortals.
> He will dwell with them;
> they will be his peoples,
> and God himself will be with them;
> he will wipe every tear from their eyes.
> Death will be no more;
> mourning and crying and pain will be no more,
> for the first things have passed away.'
> (Revelation 21:3–4, NRSV)

This is the culmination of the identification principle. It is
where the resonant declaration of 'God with us' reaches its
culmination. Emmanuel has come and has gone, but not
in order that a temporary transaction be made. This is the
consummation of God's identification with the world. Christ
joined the human race, died in our place and rose again in
triumph on the third day. Yet this is the God who has sought
enduring relationship. 'God with us' is double-coded: present
with the world, present in the church, in that ultimate time,
God is present in the city that has always been present in the
world. 'The glory and honour of the nations will be brought
into it' (Revelation 21:26).

May our eyes be opened to see God's presence in the world
and our hands opened to serve!

And so we are part of the final movement of a symphony, a
symphony that resounds with a praise-filled vision of a creation
restored, of equilibrium re-established and of paradise regained.

There has been a wrestling in the world like the cry of a
woman in childbirth: 'The creation itself will be liberated from
its bondage to decay and brought into the glorious freedom

of the children of God. We know that the whole creation has been groaning as in the pains of childbirth right up to the present time' (Romans 8:21–22).

There is an advance guard who join in the universal longing for a future without tears and carry in themselves its thrilling anticipation. It is the birth pangs of a new day. In this present age, we hear jarring sounds of disjunction, disunity, distance and dissonance. Here we experience shame; we are hanging on in faith to how we are supposed to love and how we endure some of the ugliest things life can throw at us. Tyrants and lies have their moment but we have a story, a narrative that transcends the mocking cruelty and threatens all the cultures broken by violence and the powerful. In hope we both cry and cry out, 'There is a new world arriving and it is already at the door.'

We will walk in the streets of the city, rejoining friends and loved ones who had also chosen to be there. The reunion will be sweet but not as sweet as the face-to-face reunion with the Lord who had planned for that moment so long before. We will cry and we will laugh until laughter and crying are done. And the Creator will wipe every tear from every eye and the agony will be ancient history and but a fading memory. Astonished, we will try to remember how things were and the chequered, tortured path by which we came to be there. And we will be in a new order of things and a larger dimension of life for which life here will have been but a preparation and the entrance hall.

'Did you not know you have been bought with a price?' we shall ask each other in blinding amazement. We did not, and never could, earn righteousness and standing. Yet now, through the message of the mighty cross, we are part of the new humanity, invited to an embrace of grace.

Postscript: refocusing the mission

The title at the beginning of Part Two echoes Lenin, the hate-filled genius who a century ago embarked on revolution and asked his associates, 'What is to be done?'

Our journey is complete. We have pressed the radical implications of the identification principle: God becoming one of us, one with us, one for us.

In the light of this, our witness must be holistic. It must involve:

1. in-depth intercession
2. the anointed solidarity of proclamation and apologetic
3. transformative service
4. being the frontier-crossing new humanity in the world.

We emphasize the passion and pathos of urgent prayer. Prayer that is emotionally neutral will move neither the hearts of men and women nor of our God who calls us to stand in the gap.

We emphasize anointed solidarity and the message of the cross of Christ. Twentieth-century theology and psychology betrayed people. Deny that the atonement is where Jesus paid the price for our sins and there is no place left where the bill can be paid. Yet there is a place where we can go to clear the past away, a place where Jesus stood on our behalf and died as participant and substitute so that we can be forgiven. Leave identification at the point of empathy alone and you rob people of the God-given means of dealing with the past. If we do not proclaim that there is a divinely appointed rubbish dump, a place where we can transfer all the chaos and complication of our lives, we short-change the twenty-first century. This is biblical witness and it stresses the uniqueness of Christ and what he accomplished. There has to be at least some exclusivism to make it worthwhile following Christ.

We emphasize social action that is transformative and that makes a powerful statement: 'We want to be relevant to our local community.'

We emphasize the new humanity: being with the people, sharing their joys and sorrows. This has always been the mark of pastoral work. May that never become a dwindling art form, even as the church concentrates on growth and big new centres.

Three times Moses went up into the mountain of God. The first time he was ambushed by the presence of God. It burned into his spirit with passion on fire and left him like a bush that didn't cease from burning. Waiting in ambush was Yahweh, with a self-awareness that overshadowed the stunned man and swallowed up his self-doubt. Go back Moses. Go back, for the cry of the people has reached God and he is about to intervene. Go, but come back. And so Moses returns, sees God intervene dramatically and hitch several million people to Moses' belt. There is a longing in his soul like a fire aspiring to meet the author of fire. He has an appointment with God. To the mountain he must return. There, with the people spread out across the plain, Moses comes again. There he encounters God in blazing reality and a revelation of his holy character in a way that is about to change history. But the man must go down. He must return, for there is trouble in the camp and the sound of war. But Moses no sooner settles the insurrection than he is back. He wants to come again. He can't keep away. Like a moth drawn to the light, like a man infatuated with God, he cannot keep away. But still he has to go down.

The same theme emerges in Isaiah's blazing encounter with Yahweh.

'Who will *go* for us?' he hears, with ears that are attuned, and lips now purged, now ready to speak (Isaiah 6:8). And we hear it again in Jesus' call to his disciples (and us by extension): 'He appointed twelve . . . that they might be with him and that he might send them out to preach' (Mark 3:14).

'Come.' 'Go.'

These are the two axes around which twenty-first-century spirituality must move. We need 'come' movements in our individual walk with God that will see us either return again and again to the mountain or leave us nostalgic for its fire. And we need 'come' in our church life: corporate experiences of meeting with the manifest presence of God out of which everything will move. With both pathos and joy, we hold out our arms and wave in those who are outside.

Refocusing the mission requires a repudiation of the polarization that has so cramped the church of Jesus. The incarnation propels us to get stuck in and cross new frontiers, demonstrating good news because it is incarnating good news, a release of empathy and rejection of dispassionate observation, recovering and applying the message of the cross, passionate intercessory prayer shaped by identification, plus living out good news in our lives and spurning mantelpiece holiness. All this before breakfast!

There is a level of response to human suffering that is distinctively Christian. Leave this out and the good news has not been brought to bear on the problem of pain. It is the identification principle. To redeem human beings, amazingly, the Creator embraced the very suffering he has allowed into the system. No-one can accuse him of non-involvement. Look closely at Jesus Christ and you will see God standing in solidarity with the world that we chose. God embraced the very suffering he allowed into the world because of freedom's perilous gift. The identification of Jesus is the answer to a suffering, sinful world: God joining the human race, dying in our place and rising again in triumph.

Notes

2 Worship (for all God's worth)

1. Editorial in the *Raleigh News and Observer*, 1930, cited at the opening of America's first memorial to lynching victims.

3 Children of the sixth day: the God of our humanity

1. W. McLaren, *Our Growing Creed: The Evangelical Faith as Developed and Re-affirmed by Current Thought* (Edinburgh: T. & T. Clark, 1912), p. 114.
2. John Calvin, 'Knowing God and Knowing Ourselves', *Institutes*, Book 1. As summarized in S. Olyott, *Truth for All Time* (London: Banner of Truth Trust, 1988).
3. Martin Luther, sermons on Genesis.
4. Calvin, *Institutes*, Book 1, ch. XV, p. 3.
5. C. Hodge, *Systematic Theology*, vol. 11 (Edinburgh: Nelson, 1872), p. 97.
6. I. Ilibigazia, *Left to Tell: One Woman's Story of Surviving the Rwandan Holocaust* (London: Hay House, 2006), p. 79.

4 The humanity of God

1. C. Gore (ed.) (1892), *Lux Mundi: A Series of Studies in the Religion of the Incarnation* (London: John Murray, 1892), p. 155.

2. From *Adversus Haereses* (*Against All Heresies*), 4.34.5–7.

3. *Works of Leo the Great*, ed. Philip Schaff (New York: Christian Publishing Co., 1886).

5 Becoming human (the manual)

1. Martin Luther, *Luther's Works: Volume 10: Lectures on the Psalms I*, ed. H. C. Oswald (St Louis, MO: Concordia Publishing House, 1974), p. 297.

2. Gregory of Nazianzus, *Fourth Theological Oration*, in *Nicene and Post-Nicene Fathers*, vol. 7, ed. W. Sanday (Peabody, MA: Hendrickson, 1994), p. 311.

3. *Against All Heresies*, 11.xxii.4.

4. *Against All Heresies*, v.praef.(ad fin.).

7 The empathy of God

1. Dr and Mrs Howard Taylor, *Hudson Taylor and the China Inland Mission: Growth of a Work of God* (Edinburgh: R. and R. Clarke, 1918), p. 89.

2. *Hudson Taylor and the China Inland Mission*, p. 89.

3. *Hudson Taylor and the China Inland Mission*, p. 89.

9 Redemption through violence: interpreting the cross

1. T. Wright, *Paul for Everyone: 2 Corinthians* (London: SPCK, 2003), p. 66.

10 Trading places: identification and exchange

1. Gregory of Nazianzus, *Orations* 4, in *Nicene and Post-Nicene Fathers*, vol. 7, ed. Philip Schaff and Henry Wace (New York: Cosimo, 2007), p. 317.

2. H. Ridderbos, *Paul: An Outline of His Theology* (London: SPCK, 1977), p. 168.
3. Though the extent of usage is disputed, archaeologists digging in Egypt uncovered a stack of bills with the Greek word *tetelestai* ('Paid in full') inscribed across each bill. 'The fourteen papyri here grouped together are receipts for various taxes paid by persons transporting goods on baggage animals from the Fayoum to Memphis, and vice versa across the desert road.' B. P. Grenfell and A. S. Hunt, *New Classical Fragments and other Greek and Latin Payri* (Oxford: Clarendon Press, 1897), p. 78.

11 Prayer and pathos: incarnation and intercession

1. T. Harris, *The Christian Minister in Earnest: A Memoir of the Rev. William Bramwell* (London: Wesleyan Methodist Bookroom, 1858).
2. Harris, *The Christian Minister in Earnest*, p. 43.

12 The power of proclamation: a new incarnational apologetic

1. B. Graham, *Just As I Am* (London: HarperCollins, 1997), p. 311.
2. D. Bonhoeffer, *Letters and Papers from Prison* (London: Fontana, 1959), 20 May, 1944, p. 151.

13 Transformative action and divine doorways

1. J. Wesley, *The Works of John Wesley*, vol. V, ed. T. Jackson (London: Wesleyan Methodist Bookroom, 1872), p. 296.
2. Jo Griffin, *The Lonely Society?* (London: Mental Health Foundation, 2010), p. 4.
3. Ecclesiastes 9:10, New King James Version.

14 The body of Christ and the new humanity

1. Brian Brock, 'Theologizing Inclusion: 1 Corinthians 12 and the Politics of the Body of Christ', *Journal of Religion, Disability and Health*, 15:4 (2011), pp. 351–376.

2. J. Vanier, *Community and Growth* (London: Darton, Longman and Todd, 2008), p. 74.

3. Kathrin Braun, 'From the Body of Christ to Racial Homogeneity: Carl Schmitt's Mobilization of "Life" against "the Spirit of Technicity"', *The European Legacy*, 17:1 (2012), pp. 1–17.